FOLKLORE
and
PSYCHOANALYSIS

FOLKLORE
and
PSYCHOANALYSIS

by Paulo de Carvalho-Neto

translated by

Jacques M. P. Wilson

University of Miami Press
Coral Gables, Florida

Translated from the second edition,
published under the title *Folklore y Psicoanálisis*.
Copyright © 1968 by Editorial Mortiz, Mexico.

This translation copyright © 1972 by
University of Miami Press
Library of Congress Catalog Card Number 70–26194
ISBN 0–87024–167–2

Manufactured in the United States of America

We are grateful to a number of individuals and publishers for permission to
reprint copyright material in this volume, including: Basic Books, Inc., for
material excerpted from *Three Essays on the Theory of Sexuality* by Sigmund
Freud, translated and newly edited by James Strachey, © 1962 Sigmund Freud
Copyrights Ltd: Basic Books, Inc., Publishers, New York, as well as for material
from the *Standard Edition of the Complete Psychological Works of Sigmund
Freud*. We acknowledge Sigmund Freud Copyrights Ltd, The Institute of
Psycho-Analysis and The Hogarth Press Ltd for permission to quote from
"Papers on Metapsychology" in Volume XIV of *The Standard Edition of the
Complete Works of Sigmund Freud*, revised and edited by James Strachey. For
material from *A General Introduction to Psychoanalysis* by Sigmund Freud we
acknowledge permission of Liveright, Publishers, N.Y. Copyright © Renewed
1963 by Joan Riviere, as well as Sigmund Freud Copyrights Ltd, London.

In memory of
Arthur Ramos, teacher and friend

Contents

Foreword

Although there has been considerable interest in folklore on the part of psychiatrists, there has been little or no corresponding interest in psychiatry on the part of folklorists. This is unfortunate inasmuch as folklore understood as traditional fantasy could be shown to be one of the most fascinating pieces of the picture of man. Psychiatrists have made important discoveries about the nature of folklore, but they often work at a disadvantage since they lack expertise in the discipline of folkloristics. They frequently assume, for example, that the Grimm version of an international tale type is the normal form of the tale whereas in fact it may not be at all. Also, for the most part psychiatrists have failed to study the folklore of most of the non-European peoples, preferring instead to return again and again to classical Greek mythology, favorite Bible stories, or the Grimm canon.

Folklorists as a group tend to be biased in favor of literal, not symbolic, interpretations of folklore. They seek historical rather than psychological explanations of folkloristic phenomena. There is nothing wrong with seeking historical answers to historical questions, but to ignore the fantastic dimensions of fairy tales, customs, games, etc., is to avoid asking fundamental questions as to why a given item of folklore was created in the first place or why it continues to be told or performed. Just as Stith Thompson specifically omitted "thousands of obscene motifs" from his monumental attempt to classify the elements of the world's oral literature (cf. Motif X700, Humor concerning sex, in the *Motif-Index of Folk Literature*) so all the major folklore theorists have scrupulously ignored any consideration of most of the earthy and symbolic content of folklore. They dehumanize folklore by treating *lore* as though it had nothing whatever to do with *folk*. In the standard conventional survey works purporting to treat the intellectual history of folkloristics, e.g., Giuseppe Cocchiara, *Storia del Folklore in Europa* (Torino, 1952); Inger M. Boberg, *Folkemindeforskningens Historie* (Copenhagen, 1953), one finds not so much as a mention of psychoanalysis and the possibilities of its relevance to folkloristic data. If it is mentioned, e.g., in Richard M. Dorson, "Current Folklore Theories," *Current Anthropology*, 4 (1963), 93–112, it is only for the purpose of contemptuously sneering at it or summarily dismissing it. Most folklorists would agree with Archer Taylor's assessment: "The endeavors to solve the mystery of folktales by the even more puzzling mysteries of psychoanalysis can now be laid on the shelf to gather dust" ("Some Trends and Problems in Studies of the Folk-Tale," *Studies in Philology*, 37 [1940], 17.)

In this context, it is quite remarkable that a ranking Latin American folklorist would be so bold as to attempt a book bringing together the two fields of psychoanalysis and folklore. Yet Paulo de Carvalho wrote such a book and to this day it stands as the only book-length work written by a folklorist which seriously considers in detail the psychoanalytic approach to folklore. A pioneering effort, its translation into English will hopefully widen the horizons of future generations of English-speaking folklorists.

Folklore and Psychoanalysis was first published in 1956, which means that scholarship since that time is not considered. Carvalho-Neto's book leans heavily upon the earlier, essentially classic Freudian writings. In this Carvalho-Neto follows the example of his mentor Arthur Ramos, whose own *Estudos de Folk-Lore* had previously explored some of the possible ramifications of the application of psychoanalytic insights to folklore.

A possible difficulty for some readers is the fact that Carvalho-Neto chose not to assume that the reader necessarily already possessed much familiarity with Freud or Jung's work. Consequently, several chapters (III and IV) are rather elementary paraphrases of basic concepts of psychoanalysis and analytical psychology. Readers sophisticated in psychiatry may elect to skip these chapters and go directly to the fascinating folklore case study materials. Even though these materials are presented in a rather doctrinaire

Freudian developmental order—oral, anal, genital, etc.—the examples, coming as many of them do from Brazilian sources, are likely to be of great interest. Psychiatrists will be intrigued by Carvalho-Neto's citation and analysis of Brazilian folklore even though they may find his interpretation of psychoanalytic theory somewhat dated.

After exposure to Carvalho-Neto's unique introduction to the application of psychoanalysis to folklore, many may wish to read further. Helpful general survey essays include: Weston La Barre, "Folklore and Psychology," *Journal of American Folklore*, 61 (1948), 382–390; and J. L. Fischer, "The Sociopsychological Analysis of Folktales," *Current Anthropology*, 4 (1963), 235–295.

For representative Jungian studies, see C. G. Jung and C. Kerényi, *Essays on a Science of Mythology* (New York, 1953); C. G. Jung, *Man and His Symbols* (New York, 1968); Erich Neumann, *The Origins and History of Consciousness* (New York, 1954); and Marie Louise Von Franz, *An Introduction to the Interpretation of Fairy Tales* (New York: Spring Publications, 1970). Discussions by folklorists include: Wilson M. Hudson, "Jung on Myth and the Mythic," in *The Sunny Slopes of Long Ago*, Texas Folklore Society Publications XXXIII (Dallas, 1966), pp. 181–197; Carlos C. Drake, "Jung and His Critics," *Journal of American Folklore*, 80 (1967), 321–333; and "Jungian Psychology and Its Uses in Folklore," *Journal of American Folklore*, 82 (1969), 122–131.

For representative Freudian studies, see Sigmund Freud and D. E. Oppenheim, *Dreams in Folklore* (New York, 1958); Ernest Jones, *Essays in Applied Psychoanalysis*, Vol. II, Essays in Folklore, Anthropology and Religion (London, 1951); Géza Róheim, *The Gates of the Dream* (New York, 1969). A useful discussion is Weston La Barre, "The Influence of Freud on Anthropology," *American Imago*, 15 (1958), 275–328. Anyone seriously interested in gaining access to the considerable literature dealing with the application of psychoanalysis to folklore is strongly urged to consult Alexander Grinstein's indispensable multi-volume bibliographical aid, *Index of Psychoanalytic Writings*, 9 volumes (New York, 1956–1966).

No doubt many readers will find Carvalho-Neto's book both stimulating and irritating. Some of his views on folklore are unquestionably controversial. An example would be his conclusion that there are two kinds of folklore: "usable folklore," which can be used positively for nationalistic or esthetic purposes, and "useless folklore," which should be eradicated by educators. This distinction is not shared by most folklorists. The idea that some folklore is "bad" and should be stamped out, a thesis which Carvalho-Neto develops at some length in his *Folklore y Educación* (Quito, 1961), virtually suggests that there should be some enlightened despot whose wisdom is sufficient to distinguish "good" from "bad" folklore and who can effectively eliminate the bad. It is hard to reconcile a psychoanalytic approach to folklore with the notion that certain folklore can be labeled as "bad" or the suggestion that certain traditional fantasy could possibly be curbed by imposed censorship. One of the inherent characteristics of folklore is its freedom from conscious regulation. One can attempt to control what is printed, but hardly what is said in private. In any case, even if one disagrees with Carvalho-Neto at one point or another, one can only be grateful to him for his having raised the many issues that he does. A book which makes one think and encourages discussion is a worthwhile book. Paulo de Carvalho-Neto, one of Latin America's most distinguished and prolific folklorists, has written such a book.

ALAN DUNDES

Berkeley, California

Preface to the Spanish Edition

Psychoanalytical interpretation poses a grave danger for the field of folklore. A psychoanalytical interpretation can always be developed without really proving or even confirming its value. The medical doctor who analyzes a patient will eventually know whether or not he is prescribing in accordance with the truth. The psychiatrist can correct or modify his hypotheses after several sessions by exposing them to new events, new dreams, or new free associations. The cure is further proof of the validity of his interpretation. But in the realm of folklore where there is scarcely more than the reading of a tale or an account of a custom or traditional chronicle, new questions cannot be asked and it is never known whether what was stated was true or false. There is an ease of interpretation here which is very unfortunate. It is true that a study needs a hypothesis, but when there is no possibility of proof, there is not much left that can be called science.

This opinion does not refute the efforts undertaken by Paulo de Carvalho-Neto who followed the path indicated by his professor, Arthur Ramos. Those who wish to read my study, *Sociology and Psychoanalysis*, will see that I believe in the value of the psychoanalytical method. I only wish to warn the reader and to advise him to use this method cautiously. In any case I feel that a psychoanalysis of folklore should finish with a discussion of the logical problem of proof. Abraham Kardiner's value rests on his having attempted to do so. He considers folklore as a projection of complexes and cultural traumas. Kardiner does not study folklore in isolation but rather relates it to the education of individuals, their social development, and the restraints of infancy which are revealed by ethnography. In addition he uses life histories and Rorschach tests. Psychoanalytical interpretation is only acceptable to the extent that the hypothetical analysis of folklore coincides with the psychology of the individual. If our interpretation of a legend contradicts the results of a Rorschach test or educational norms imposed on children, our interpretation probably has no more than a tenuous relation to the true meaning of the legend. Another interpretation has to be found.

This method, unfortunately, is only valid for the peoples we call "primitive." How can we prove the validity of the interpretation of tales, legends, and taboos which have come to us from a distant past and perhaps no longer reflect our complexes? For my part, I only see one method, that of tests. In the past I used them when studying the role of social groups in transmitting legends, their transformation by neglect and by the increase or change of the themes. It seems to me that an analogous method could be found for psychoanalytical interpretation. But this proof would require a very difficult and carefully prepared study. It would require that a number of groups of people be psychoanalyzed—people governed by oral, anal, and oedipal complexes, for example. They would all be told a little known or unknown tale with anal characteristics borrowed from a foreign mythology. If in transmittal the anal group sets aside some of the symbols we feel are the characteristics of the anal structure of the tale, then there is a strong probability that our interpretation of the mythology as anal is erroneous. On the contrary, however, forgetfulness may function as the resistance of the individual to his own libido. A series of psychoanalytical sessions around the omitted theme would let us know whether resistance or unintentional forgetfulness was present. Resistance would be proof supporting our interpretation while unintentional forgetfulness would be proof against us. The remaining groups, functioning as controls, would also provide us with favorable or unfavorable signs. The process is costly and difficult. But the rules of logic always require us to seek the proof of our hypothesis. Science, no matter which one, cannot be developed in any other way.

Psychoanalysis, when well conceived, leads us to seek the same conclusion. We know, for example, that there is no key meaning for oneiric symbols. The same object has a different meaning for each individual. Thus the symbols do not explain the neurosis, but rather the neurosis allows the discovery of the variable meanings of the symbols. In a word, it is always necessary to study the life of the individual for a frame of reference. The same is true for folklore. Its analysis must ascertain its foundation, and its proof must rest on the analysis of individuals: those who believe it, those who pass it on, and those who modify it.

ROGER BASTIDE

Introduction

The objective of this work is to systematize the relationship of folklore and psychoanalysis and to examine what I call "interdisciplinary folklore" in one of its fundamental aspects. I began with the work of my professor, Arthur Ramos. I felt it appropriate to use his examples, so this study could also be considered "a detailed systematization of the psychoanalytical folklore in the studies of Arthur Ramos."

In spite of the hypothetical nature of the relationship between these two disciplines, this study tries to provide methodical arrangement, judgment, and clarity. Many colleagues have testified to its value. If tacit approval on the part of my closest scholarly colleagues had been insufficient to motivate me to prepare this edition, two events which occurred after the publication of the first edition (1956) would have been. One was a resolution of the Fifth Brazilian Folklore Congress which met in Fortaleza, Ceará, in July 1963. It stated: "Folkloric datum is subject to interpretation by psychologists. It is felt that the symbolic interpretation provided by psychoanalysis is an attempt at interpretation." The second event was the program of the Third Latin American Congress of Psychiatry which met in Lima in 1964. "Folkloric Psychiatry" was included on its agenda and this is contiguous with psychoanalytical folklore.

P. DE CARVALHO-NETO

Part One: History

A Brief Survey

The first attempt in Latin America to develop the history of the relationship between folklore and psychoanalysis was undertaken by Arthur Ramos. He did so near the end of his life in an excellent chapter in his *Estudos de Folklore* entitled "Psychoanalytical Theories" (56:140–153). In it he mentions the forerunners and considers the following authors: M. L. W. Laistner, E. Clodd, W. Golther, S. Freud, F. Riklin, K. Abraham, O. Rank, H. Silberer, C. G. Jung, and E. Jones. He refers to them as classics of analytical demopsychology even though his discussion of them is brief.

Ramos' synthesis of the above scholars does not need amplification, but merely to be enriched by the addition of other contributors: B. Malinowski, J. P. Porto-Carrero, E. Carneiro, A. Kardiner, R. Bastide, M. Langer, B. Canal-Feijoo, and J. Wortis. Some of them were never mentioned by Ramos; others like Kardiner and Malinowski were included in his plans when death overtook him. At the proper point Ramos' own contribution to Latin American psychoanalytical folklore will be summarized. The system he used in producing his synthesis has been slightly modified, but in the main the original has been followed.

The relation between folklore and psychoanalysis has been noted since the time of the hermeneutic Greeks. The principal advance, however, was made as a result of the anthropological theories of the nineteenth century. These theories developed explanations for the existence of certain folkloric phenomena through the study of the human psyche—for example, Adolf Bastian's *Elementargedanken*, the English anthropological school (Tylor, Lang, and

Frazer), Theodule Armand Ribot's affective psychology, and the French school of anthropology led by Lucien Lévy-Bruhl.

The immediate radius of influence of these theories was considerable. Eugenio Tanzi, for example, found characteristic traces of primitive mentality among the insane. Ramos writes, "According to Tanzi, the rantings of the paranoid are nothing more than the more or less faithful reproduction of psychological formulas normally characteristic of the savage" (63:36). Tanzi was thus able to call folklore to the attention of psychiatrists. Furthermore, according to Vicenzo Grossi, his predecessor, the remains of primitive intelligence and the elements of sick or deviant intelligences should be found in folklore (59:317). Ramos states that "Tanzi was careful to point out that although paranoid behavior imitated that of the savage, it was not identical. It is not a faithful reproduction since the savages were 'children of their times,' while paranoids are 'counterfeit contemporaries,' that is to say, chronologically dislocated, real living anachronisms." Tanzi stated that the primitive's mysticism is the modest, quiet, and collective manifestation of an imperfect mind which is developing. The mysticism of paranoids is the audacious, violent, and individual explosion of a regressive and antisocial mind (63:39–40).

Because of these and similar statements, Tanzi must be considered as much a forerunner of psychoanalytical folklore as Bastian, Tylor, Ribot, and Lévy-Bruhl. Among Tanzi's work Ramos recommends: *La paranoia e la sua evoluzione storica* (1844), *I neologismi degli alienati in rapporto col delirio cronico* (1889), *Il folklore nella patologia mentale* (1890), *The Germ of Delirium* (1891), and *Sopravvivenze psichiche* (1891).

LAISTNER, CLODD, AND GOLTHER: NIGHTMARES AND FOLKLORE

Although not included by Ramos among the forerunners of folklore, Max L. W. Laistner, Edward Clodd, and Wolfgang W. Golther antedate psychoanalysis as a science and are suitable material for the history of psychoanalytical folklore. In his *Das Rätsel der Sphinx* (1889), Laistner tried to prove that mythology originated in dreams and primarily in nightmares. Clodd in turn continued the line of this thesis when he wrote *Myths and Dreams* (1891) and concluded likewise that "we owe largely [to nightmares] the creation of the vast army of nocturnal demos that inhabit the world's folklore." Finally, Golther was even more specific when he affirmed that in matters of folklore the result of nightmares is a belief in spirits. His *Handbuch der germanischen Mythologie* (1895) dealt with this topic.

SIGMUND FREUD: PHYLOGENETIC SYMBOLISM

It was left to Freud's now famous *The Interpretation of Dreams* (1901) to demonstrate what is, in Ramos' opinion, the real meaning of the analogy between dreams and myths. Ramos indicated that the discovery of oneiric symbols brought them together. Furthermore, he felt that dreams employ symbolic images, that is, specific figures which take the place of other subconscious ideas which then need to be interpreted. But these symbols are not the exclusive property of the dreamer. They are a type of subconscious collective patrimony which is verifiable in the plebeian psyche, in myths, in legends, and in proverbs. The symbolism is then phylogenetic in the majority of cases: it results from the accumulated experience of generations. Freud indicated that this symbolism does not belong exclusively to dreams but is an unconscious idea belonging to the populace and revealed more intelligibly in folklore, myths, legends, idioms, proverbs, and the ordinary anecdotes of a people. Ramos continues by quoting the head of the Vienna school when the latter affirms in his *Introduction to Psychoanalysis* (1916–1918) that the understanding of the meaning of symbols is unknown to the dreamer himself: "For we have discovered that the same symbolism is employed in myths and fairy tales, in popular sayings and songs, in colloquial speech and poetic phantasy. The province of symbolism is extraordinarily wide: dream symbolism is only a small part of it; it would not even be expedient to attack the whole problem from the side of dreams. Many of the symbols commonly occurring elsewhere either do not appear in dreams at all or appear very seldom; on the other hand, many of the dream symbols are not met with in every other department but only here and there. We get the impression that here we have to do with an ancient but obsolete mode of expression, of which different fragments have survived in different fields, one here only, another there only, a third in various spheres perhaps in slightly different forms" (4:144).

Through the discovery of the Oedipus complex, a basic complex in psychoanalysis, Freud also opened new horizons for interpretive studies of folklore. In fact, with this complex he accomplished the first mythographic psychoanalytical interpretation using as an archetype the Greek legend of King Oedipus, handed down across the ages by the scholarly versions of Sophocles and Euripedes. He even reached conclusions concerning crimes which survive in totemism and on which social institutions for the control of primitive communities are based.

After Freud many writers stand out for having applied psychoanalysis to the interpretation of folkloric acts in a general way. Franz Riklin, Karl Abraham, Otto Rank, Herbert Silberer, Carl G. Jung, and Ernest Jones are among those who have studied the analogies between dreams and myths.

FRANZ RIKLIN: FAIRY TALES AND THE "REALIZATION OF DESIRES"

In his *Wunscherfüllung und Symbolik im Märchen* (1908) Franz Riklin again treated the Freudian concept of the dream and attempted to prove that dreams, symbolism, and the "realization of desires" *(Wunscherfüllung)* in plebeian tales are governed by the same laws. Ramos says that "Historically Riklin's work is the first to apply the psychoanalytical method to folklore. The mechanisms of the dream, the various oneiric processes for the fashioning of dreams—that is, condensation *(Verdichtung)*, displacement *(Verschiebung)*, dramatization *(Darstellung)*, and symbolism *(Symbolik)*—can all be found in the fable and in the tales of the populace, which need interpretation and explication of their hidden meanings. It is the discovery of the latter absurd element which so preoccupies mythographers. . . . The realization of desires in tales is evident, according to Franz Riklin, in those series of fantasies realized by characters in adventures: marriage to charmed princes, the conquest of love and fortune, and the triumph of good over

evil. . . . Condensation and displacement explain the magical transformations, the hallucinatory metamorphoses, the totality of the
might of the dramatis personae of the tale. Love potions and sorcerers fill the scenes of popular tales. All the basic complexes found
in dreams and neurosis by psychoanalysts are also the motives of
the tale and the myth" (56:145).

KARL ABRAHAM: MORE ON DREAMS AND MYTHS

Karl Abraham developed the already familiar psychological
parallel between the dream and the myth in his *Traum und Mythus* (1909) one year after Franz Riklin. Among other things he
inferred that the myth contains in a disguised way the childish
desires of a people and that the myth is a surviving fragment of
the infantile mental state of a people, while the dream is the
individual's myth. In other words, the myth is the populace's
dream, while the dream is the individual's myth. The same rules
governing dreams—condensation, displacement, and disguise—are
found in the myth (56:146).

Paraphrasing the psychoanalytical interpretation of the Oedipus
story, Abraham developed a similar interpretation of the Prometheus myth. According to his version, Promethean fire is the fire
of love, generic love, and Prometheus is the rebel son who wishes
to steal his father's sexual attributes and is punished for it (a central theme of psychoanalysis). Abraham finds similar meaning in
the myth of Samson and Delilah. When Delilah takes away Samson's strength by cutting his hair, it is a symbolic castration. In
other words, the hero is stripped of his phallic attributes.

OTTO RANK: THE HERO

According to Ramos, psychoanalytical mythography reached a
new stage with Otto Rank because of the originality of his contribution. Rank applied the discoveries of psychoanalysis not only
to the interpretation of myths but to legends, plebeian tales, and
artistic productions in a basic series of studies beginning with the
essay titled *Der Mythus von der Geburt des Helden* (1909). Like

Abraham, who amplified the Freudian interpretation of the Oedipus myth, Rank discovered new dimensions in the stories of Sargon, Moses, Paris, Romulus, Herod, Jesus, Sigfried, Lohengrin, and many other myths and legends about saints, gods, and heroes. In his opinion the following generally occurs:

1. The hero is always the son of a king or of noble parents. His gestation and birth are surrounded by mystery.
2. The father is a tyrant, a dreadful parent who wishes to suppress or kill the son.
3. The latter is abandoned in a mysterious place, generally the waters of a river where he is found by poor parents or reared by a humble woman or even by animals.
4. The hero grows up and one day finds the tyrant father and avenges himself by killing him. He is then raised to the paternal state, is feasted as a hero or adored as a god (59:149).

According to Otto Rank this plan contains many psychoanalytical mechanisms among which are infantile fantasies about parents and fantasies about birth.

After *Der Mythus von der Geburt des Helden,* Rank published the following works: *Die Lohengrinsage* (1911), *Der Sinn der Griseldafabel* (1912), *Das Inzestmotiv in Dichtung und Sage* (1912), *Die Bedeutung der Psychoanalyse für die Geisteswissenschaften* (1913), *Die Nacktheit in Dichtung und Sage* (1913), *Totemismus im Märchen* (1913), *Psychoanalytische Beiträge zur Mythenforschung* (1919), *Das Traum der Geburt und seine Bedeutung für die Psychoanalyse* (1924), *Der Künstler* (5th ed., 1925), and others, such as, *Traum and Dichtung* and *Traum und Mythus.*

In these other works Rank examines the presence of other psychoanalytical mechanisms in folkloric narratives such as those surrounding the incest motive: possession of the mother, hatred of the father, punishment (mutilation, castration), and the expiation of the offense (56:151).

HERBERT SILBERER: FUNCTIONAL SYMBOLISM

Herbert Silberer enriched the field of psychoanalytical folklore with new interpretations of myths and plebeian tales in the following works: *Von den Kategorien der Symbolik* (1910), *Über die Symbolbildung* (1911), *Phantasie und Mythus* (1911), *Über Märchensymbolik* (1912), and *Zur Symbolbildung* (1912). Furthermore, he seems to have discovered the motive for mutilation (of the hero) and developed his own theory of symbolism, the so-called functional symbolism which is used in combination with the concept of anagogical interpretation (56:151).

CARL JUNG: HETERODOX

Dissidents from the Freudian school of psychoanalytical folklore were not heard from in plain language until Carl G. Jung's masterpiece *Transformations and Symbols of the Libido* (1911) appeared. Jung began by inverting the point of departure. Instead of applying elements of individual psychology to myths (the orthodox position), he attempted to find a mythological formula in the contents *(Inhalt)* of the dream, the neurosis, and the psychosis. This difference of criteria is even pointed out by Freud in *Totem and Taboo* (1913) and by Ramos. Freud admitted that his methods differed from those of the Zurich school which attempted to explain individual psychology by data collected from mass psychology (56:151).

A second concept of Jung's deals with the psychoanalytical complexes in folklore. He claims that, in the myths he analyzed, the fundamental complexes of psychoanalysis are sublimated and desexualized. Therefore the hero's rejection of the mother should not be seen as a sign of defeat but rather of sacrifice and of triumph over the father by the destruction of all the ties which bind them together. In other words, civilization is the progressive freeing of the libidinal elements, a fact which Jung proved from the myths.

In addition to these contributions Jung developed the idea of the superindividual collective unconscious, and distinguished it from the classic individual unconscious. Ancestral images or archtypes are found in the collective unconscious, that is, images or mythological symbols of gods, demons, sages, witches, and ghosts from all time, all myths, and all folklores.

ERNEST JONES: THE ONEIRIC THEORY

Psychoanalytical folklore returned to the rigid Freudian methodology with Ernest Jones. Jones again dealt with the themes studied by Laistner, Clodd, and Golther, and broadened the oneiric theory of the origin of folklore. In his *Der Albtraum in seiner Beziehung zu gewissen Formen des mittelalterlichen Aberglaubens* (1912), he pointed out that the devils, vampires, lucifers, demons, and witches in medieval superstitions had their origin in nightmares. He even listed the common elements of nightmares and medieval superstitions, restated by Arthur Ramos as follows:

1. A sensation of anguish tied to suppressed sexual desires, many of which are of an incestuous nature.
2. The transformation of one individual into another or into some kind of animal.
3. The occurrence of fantastic types of strange animals.
4. The alternation of attractive and repulsive objects.
5. The simultaneous existence of the same individual in two different places.
6. The idea of flying or floating in space.

BRONISLAW MALINOWSKI: ANTHROPOLOGICAL CRITICISM

Everything that is critical of psychoanalysis, whether from anthropology or other fields, is of intense interest to psychoanalytical folklore. This is why Bronislaw Malinowski can not be omitted from this overview.

Malinowski was born in Cracow, Poland. He died suddenly in 1942 while professor of anthropology at Yale University. In a large measure his criticism of psychoanalysis stems from his field trips to the Trobriand Islands in the South Pacific. These trips provided material for *The Sexual Life of Savages* (1929), *Sex and Repression in Savage Society* (1927), *The Myth in Primitive Society* (1926), and *The Family Among the Australian Aborigines* (1913). The latter monograph is of particular interest.

Malinowski's important discovery in the Trobriand Islands was that the family unit there was fundamentally different from the one Freud investigated in Vienna. Consequently, the universal validity which Freud sought to give to the Oedipus complex was refuted. Although not denying the complex categorically, Malinowski found that it was altered by the family structure: Freud's Viennese family was patriarchal, while the Trobriand family in Malinowski's study was matriarchal.

Malinowski characterizes the family Freud studied as an Indo-European family, that is, a patrilineal family with a well-defined sense of paternal authority, reinforced by Roman law, Christian morality, and the modern European industrialism of the wealthy bourgeoisie. On the other hand, Freud was not acquainted with the matriarchal family of the Trobriands in which parental authority is derived exclusively from the mother and in which rights of succession and inheritance are governed by the maternal line. Furthermore, in this system the father is a beloved and benevolent friend but not a relative of the children in any recognized sense of the word, and the mother's brother embodies the principle of discipline and authority. The nuclear complexes of these two types of families are as different as are (logically) their influence on the formation of myths, legends, and tales.

To add support to his thesis Malinowski dedicates the greater part of his study to Trobriand ethnography by treating the various cycles of the individual's life span: lactation (1-3 years), childhood (5-8 years), adolescence (9-15 years). The final chapter contains a synthesis and conclusions. He indicates, for example, that infant rivalries and subsequent social functions introduce a certain amount of animosity and ill-will into the father-son relationship in a patriarchal society. The premature separation of the son from his mother rouses deep and insatiable desires which later, when sexual interests develop, frequently take on a neurotic character, revealing themselves in dreams or other fantasies and mingling with the new physical appetites. Such friction, however, does not occur between the Melanesian father and son. All infantile appetite for the mother is gradually and naturally exhausted without restriction. The ambivalence of veneration and hatred is vented against the mother's brother. At this time such repressed incestuous temptations for sexual relations which may appear are only realized with the sister.

Classifying both social structures briefly and rather roughly, Malinowski states that our suppressed desire to kill the father and marry the mother lies in the Oedipus complex, while among the inhabitants of the Trobriand Islands, whose social structure is matrilineal, it is characterized by the expectation of marrying one's sister and killing the mother's brother. These conclusions are important since the possibility of a different type of nuclear complex was never imagined until then (49).

Malinowski thus confirms the main lines while modifying the details of Freudian psychology. His studies establish that Freud's theories agree with general human psychology, but that they can be specifically adapted to account for the changes that different social forms produce in human nature. That is, he demonstrates the intimate relationship existing between a designated type of society and its corresponding nuclear complex. Although Malinowski finds remarkable support for the principle of Freudian psychology, he indicates the need to modify some of its details or provide some of its concepts with greater elasticity. The reciprocal relationship between the biological and social influences needed to be researched and while he does not confirm the general validity of the Oedipus complex, Malinowski advocates the separate study of each cultural type with the object of identifying its unique complex.

This doubtlessly coincides with the logical principle which condemns the study of man in the abstract, as did Freud—that is, the study of "man in general," not as a part of a particular whole, but equally a part of Viennese society as of Trobriand. Defending the idea of studying man specifically, of each established culture, and proposing an integral and functional method, Malinowski characterizes himself as one of the many anthropologists with a dialectical education.

The path he followed in the ethno-psychological essay defined the influence of the family type on the nuclear complex and that of the latter on folklore. It is a path which, when put in a formula, can be outlined as follows: economic organization → type of society → psychic reactions → folklore.

Emphasizing that the influences affecting folklore among the Trobrianders are produced by their kind of society Malinowski, states that Melanesian folklore generally reflects the matrilineal family. When we examine the myths, tales, and legends, as well as Melanesian magic, we see the repressed hatred of the mother's brother normally hidden by veneration and the sentiments of community. It is seen in their fables as daydreams dictated by repressed desires (49). Ramos discusses these statements of Malinowski primarily in his *O folklore negro do Brasil* (57:29) and *Introdução à Psicologia Social* (59:272).

ABRAHAM KARDINER: A SYNTHESIS

It should be understood that the position one takes with respect to psychoanalytical folklore depends on what point of view is taken with respect to psychoanalysis and dialectical materialism. It is not a cause but an effect.

In the Soviet Union the hypotheses of psychoanalytical folklore are not honored because, although folklore is, psychoanalysis is not permitted in that country. As Joseph Wortis well observes, psychoanalysis is not even practiced; what prevails in every system of thought is historical or dialectical materialism. Materialism takes total possession of folklore. Any possibility at all of a humble psychoanalytical attempt at understanding is proscribed. This is the typical orthodoxy of Sokolov, Gorky, and Carneiro. The converse is true in most other countries: pure psychoanalysis without the slightest hint of materialist intervention.

At last the syncretic writers appeared. William Reich, Erich Fromm, R. Osborn, J. F. Brown, Burrill Freedman, J. B. Furst, Judson T. Stone, and others tried to reconcile psychoanalysis and dialectical materialism (69:90). Then Bronislaw Malinowski, Abraham Kardiner, Ralph Linton, Ruth Benedict, Margaret Mead, and, even though he would not admit it, Arthur Ramos applied these eclectic efforts to the relationship between psychoanalytical folklore and dialectical materialism.

In my opinion Ramos always belonged to the syncretic group. He was a materialist dedicated to psychoanalytical folklore and never exclusively a folkloric psychoanalyst without a materialist outlook. In other words, he was never classically Freudian.

In 1939 Abraham Kardiner, a professor at Columbia University, published his work *The Individual and His Society* with the following subtitle: *The Psychodynamics of Primitive Social Organization.* This extensive work is divided into three parts: methodology, description, and theory. In the first, the author analyzes the socioanthropological concepts he uses, ideas about culture, and basic disciplines. In the second, he applies the basic principles to two aboriginal cultures. In the third, he traces the history of psychoanalytical social psychology, pointing out the most important principles and demonstrating the application of the psychopathological technique to the problems of sociology. It is in this third part that Kardiner unleashes his criticism of Freud.

Freud's principal error, according to Kardiner, was to study man in the abstract and without prior reference to a specific culture. This is a mistake of evolutionism. Anthropology was evolutionist in Freud's time and in using it for his studies leading to *Totem and Taboo* the author of depth psychology did nothing more than introduce evolutionism to psychoanalysis. Kardiner, on the other hand, defends the detailed study of cultures, since he believes that cultures must be studied as units (45:14).

Another Freudian error, according to Kardiner, was to consider the action of the psyche over the environment as a determinative factor while leaving out reciprocal action. It is not by chance that the Oedipus complex does not exist in the Marquesas Islands, but rather it is because "the social organization which originated it among the Tanalas was absent in the other culture" (45:410). What is more important is the culture: folklore depends on it. "Folklore is characteristic only of the group which creates it, and even if tales are appropriated by diffusion, they are rapidly changed to conform to the new conditions under which the adapters of the tale live." In other words, "as institutions change, so do the products of fantasy of those who live under them" (45:417, 107). This principle is completely dialetic and Carneiro states it even more succinctly: "In fact, folkloric forms correspond to determined social forms and are modified or disappear in accordance with this correspondence" (9:11).

Since folklore is thus an expression of each culture as a functional unit, it can not even be used as a historical guide. Kardiner adds, "If we dismiss folklore as an accurate historical guide and attribute to it only functional significance, then we have severed one tie with historical reconstructions. . . . Folklore may contain elements of history; but what is historical in it is of relatively little importance, because the history is distorted to the use of expressing current conflicts—conflicts of a general kind created by the existing social organization—but retaining nothing of the remote past, except perhaps the characters" (45:107–108).

A third Freudian error was to overvalue the phylogenetic over the ontogenetic, that is, to attempt to explain events taking place in the individual's life by the history of the human species (45:403–404). This was an error shared by Jung who, although disagreeing with him on other aspects, began with this principle in the development of the concept of the collective unconscious. The profitable criticism of the Columbia professor did not stop there. We have only pointed out here those aspects which in our opinion bear closely on psychoanalytical folklore. In summary:

1. Kardiner urges the study of psychoanalytical folklore by cultures as functional units and he rejects evolutionist studies.
2. He adopts this position primarily because he considers that the infrastructure determines the superstructure without excluding reciprocal influences.
3. From this he infers that it is senseless to study history through folklore since the latter reveals more about the present than the past. It is derived from the present patterns of society, although it may at times contain the names of historical characters.

This is perhaps the meaning which should be given to Sokolov's statement that "Folklore is the echo of the past, but at the same time it is the powerful voice of the present." Gorky was more extreme when he stated that "it is not only the creation of the past and the present, but also of the future" (9:29, 31, 32).

4. Kardiner concludes that the idea of cultural atavism which may exist hereditarily in the individual cannot be justified.

As a result of what has been stated, I do not believe that I am mistaken in placing Kardiner among the group of psychoanalytical anthropologists who use the method of dialectical materialism. He suggested that once these difficulties had been clarified (referring to the difficulties placed in evidence by dialectical materialism) the powerful tools of psychoanalysis must be regrouped to develop new methods for their utilization. This was the position which informed his monumental work.

Because of his exceptional scientific and scholarly energy, Kardiner attempted to provide original solutions to these problems and in so doing developed a method which can well be called the

Kardiner method. It is a method based fundamentally on the descriptive and comparative study of cultures. Its seed has begun to bear fruit, such as the interesting study of Carmen Viqueira and Angel Palerm "Alcoholismo, brujería y homicidio en dos comunidades rurales de México."

JOSEPH WORTIS: MARXIST CRITIC

In this brief history we still need to consider the Marxist criticism of psychoanalysis in order to obtain a more concrete idea of the status of psychoanalytical folklore in socialist countries. This is provided by Joseph Wortis, an American psychiatrist of Russian origin, in his study *Soviet Psychiatry* (1950):

1. Dialectical materialism teaches that "Mind is a function of matter and is derivative from and secondary to it" (69:2). Matter in turn, is conditioned by economics. Economics (the infrastructure) is consequently the basis for the mind's (superstructure) behavior. Freud dismisses this principle, subjecting the economic to the libido, and even explains the former by the latter with his theory of the anal complex.

2. This leads Freudians to an ultra-individualistic position, one of purely subjective idealism, since individuals explain society rather than the converse being the case. This is to say, Freud does not explain the behavior of individuals as the product of group struggles, but, on the contrary, he regards social life as the mechanistic sum of the behavior of individuals (69:77).

3. This reasoning is understood better when it is clear that for the Freudian the conscious is governed by the unconscious. The environment directly influences the conscious (ego), but since the later is subordinate to the unconscious id, the environment's influence on the individual is almost nil. This cannot be countenanced by Marxists since they seek to change the world by controlled education.

4. Dialectical materialism affirms among its basic principles that "no phenomenon in nature exists by itself, in isolation, but everything is dependent on context, connections, and relations to other things" (69:2). Because of this, Marxist analyses endeavor to be concrete in specific situations and areas. Freud, on the other hand, developed his entire theory on man in the abstract sense, "man

in general." Man can live as well under the socialist socioeconomic conditions as capitalist ones, conditions which are radically different from each other. This is one of the reasons why psychoanalysis is considered antiscientific, idealistic, and metaphysical by the Marxists: Freudianism places itself above social classes.

5. Materialist causality is immediate and mediate. It is not so mediate, however, as to allow the explanations of adulthood by childhood as is the case in psychoanalysis.

6. Psychoanalysis is deterministic. Soviet man would become disheartened as a result of its concepts, since he would discover that his revolutionary struggle for a better country is nothing more, fundamentally, than hatred for his father (4:160).

7. The true significance of psychoanalysis is that it is a product of the western world. Its perseverance is explained by "its usefulness to scientific lackeys of the ruling classes who utilize it for the purpose of concealing the real contradictions which beset a class society" (69:101). Or, according to Vnukov, "It must be stated directly that the only true evaluation of psychoanalysis is to consider it as a fragment of bourgeois democracy" (69:76).

In conclusion we can state concerning psychoanalysis that Marxism is characterized as explaining the superstructure by the infrastructure, deriving the behavior of individuals from the group's efforts and struggles, and considering the conscious independent from the deep unconscious. When a specific man is studied, his childhood means much less than adulthood and his values of will, faith, and hope are just and true. In turn Freudianism subordinates the economic to the libido and explains society through the individuals who make it up. The conscious is always in the grip of the unconscious, this principle being true for each and every man. To understand him it is better to go back to his childhood than to pause and consider the present: to consider his apparently noble actions as the result of unmentionable disgraceful impulses.

This then is the conflict between Marxism and psychoanalysis. There are many other points worth noting but those already mentioned give us a precise idea of why analytical demopsychology is something unacceptable in the U.S.S.R.

For this discusison Wortis used, among others, the following principal sources: A Luriïa "Pskihoanaliz," in the *Bolshaia Entsiklopediia* (1940); I. Sapir, *Freudismus, Soziologie, Psychologie: Unter dem Banner des Marxismus* (1930); V. Vnukov, "Psikhoanaliz," in the *Meditsinkaia Entsiklopediia* (1933); K. Veide-miuller and A. Shchelgov, "Freudizm," in the *Bolshaia Entsiklopediia* (1935); S. L. Rubinstein, *Osnovy obschei psikhologii* (1946); M. D. Gurevich and M. I. Sereiskii, *Uchebnik psikhiatrii* (1946); and V. Kolbanovskii, "Za Marksistkoe osveschenie voprosov psikhologii," in *Bolshevik* (1947).

He does not neglect to include those who attempt to combine Marxism with psychoanalysis to achieve a favorable synthesis. I refer to William Reich, *Dialektischer Materialismus und Psychoanalyse: Unter dem Banner des Marxismus* (1929); Erich Fromm, "Über Methode und Aufgabe einer analytischen Sozialpsychologie," in *Zeitung fur Sozialforschung* (1932); R. Osborn, *Freud and Marx, A Dialectal Study* (1937); J. F. Brown, "Freud vs. Marx," in *Psychiatry* (1938); Burrill Freedman, "Psychosocial repression and social rationalization," in the *American Journal of Orthopsychiatry* (1939); J. B. Furst, "Progressives and Psychoanalysis," in *New Masses* (1945); Judson T. Stone, "Theory and Practice of Psychoanalysis," in *Science and Society* (69:90). The most difficult problem for all these conciliators is expressed in the following quotation from Vnukov, "Those who attempted to inject Marxism into psychoanalysis ended up by being captives of psychoanalysis" (69:76).

In concluding, Wortis states that psychoanalysis is far removed from dialectical and historical materialism on questions of principle and because of that it is completely unacceptable in the U.S.S.R. where it is felt to be "representative of decadent western ideologies," "a fragmentary aspect of bourgeois democracy," and "a reactionary tendency" (69).

Although it is true that for a period of time there were Soviet defenders of psychoanalysis among scientific psychotherapists, they disappeared due to the popularity attained by the theories of Ivan Petrovitch Pavlov (1849–1936). Someday this partial criticism of psychoanalysis will be included in a study where criticisms from all the disciplines will be carefully recorded. We need this. They would begin with those from heterodox psychoanalysis: Jung, Adler, Karen Horney; from sociology: Sorokin, L. von Wiese, Dalbiez, Zillborg, Burgess, Bastide; from anthropology: Malinowski, Kardiner, Roheim; from literature: Emil Ludwig and his irresponsible and iconoclastic *Freud démasqué*, and so on.

Folklore in Latin America

Ramos was the true pioneer of psychoanalytical folklore in Latin America and he disseminated the theories of the German specialists throughout our profession. In Brazil there had already been Tobias Barreto who, like Ramos, without ever having been in Germany, introduced the fundamental ideas of law held by the Nordic schools.

Ramos was doubly revolutionary since he made his point by using local Brazilian folklore. Quite the contrary from what his detractors have stated, he was never dogmatic. He perceived clearly the relativity of his studies, which motivated him to work even harder with the hope of building something solid. Here is one of the passages which clearly demonstrates his conviction that his conclusions were tentative: "Certainly we must not foster the illusion that these new methods and theories are definitive and infallible. They are *nothing more than new working hypotheses.* ... They are reflections of the scientific spirit of the times which leads us to new research. We must not concern ourselves with the *truth* of a hypothesis but rather with the productiveness of its results. If science in our time denies the preciseness of certain postulates of the Nina-Rodrigues period,* we cannot therefore refuse to recognize how productive the results of his research were and continue to be" (60:29).

Unfortunately, he was never able to condense in a single volume this theoretical and practical support for psychoanalytical folklore. He did not live long enough. Death overtook him at forty six years of age and cut short his work. In reality his primary con-

*Raymundo Nina-Rodrigues was a pioneer in Brazilian black culture studies.

cern was the Brazilian Negro and he only returned to psychoanalytical folklore sporadically, almost exclusively as it pertained
to his favorite topic. To classify the work of Ramos as to the
assistance it has provided psychoanalytical folklore is to list his
works in three groups:

1. Initial phase: *Primitivo e loucura* (1926), *Estudos de psicanálise* (1931), *Freud, Adler, Jung* (1933), *Psiquiatria e psicanálise* (1933), *Educacão e psicanálise* (1934), *Loucura e crime* (1937).*

2. Mature phase (a heavy emphasis on the application of psychoanalysis to Brazil's folklore): *O Negro brasileiro* (1934), *O folklore
negro do Brasil* (1935), *Introduçã à Psicologia Social* (1936), *A organização dual entre os índios brasileiros* (1945).

3. Final phase (an outline of general psychoanalytical folklore
and that of Brazil): *Estudos de folklore* (1952).**

Material from the above works bearing on folklore and psychoanalysis will be brought together in this study. I have attempted to
amplify the third phase (which was inconclusive) to pay Ramos
an honest and dignified homage.

PÔRTO-CARRERO: DISCIPLE

Although Ramos was doubtlessly the originator of Latin American psychoanalytical folklore, he had contemporary disciples who
should be mentioned. One of them was J. P. Pôrto-Carrero. Together in the decade of 1930–1940, Ramos and Pôrto-Carrero began
to modify the classical Brazilian structure of psychology by introducing fundamental ideas from the then novel Freudian psychoanalysis. While Ramos was publishing his studies in 1931 and 1933,
his distinguished colleague was preparing *A psicologia profunda ou
psicanálise* (1932), *Criminologia e psicanálise* (1932), *Psicanálise
de uma civilização* (1933), and *Ensaios de psicanálise* (1934). Time,
however, induced them to follow different paths. Ramos embraced
the themes of psychoanalytical folklore, while Pôrto-Carrero barely
touched this topic in his very interesting chapter "Myths, Legends,
and Infantile Tales" in *A psicologia profunda ou psicanálise.*

---

*Not exactly a book but rather a collection of articles most of which were
published prior to 1934.
**A posthumous work.

Despite the fact that his contribution to psychoanalytical folklore is so small, in all justice we must mention it. The chapter mentioned above is a study of the ontophylogenetic theory, symbolism in general, and the influence of infantile sexual curiosity and the Oedipus complex on folkloric acts. We should mention the following examples from his study:

1. Fertilization: Sargon placed in a safe at the mercy of the waters; the Virgin Mother of Christianity fertilized by the divine spirit (breath), similar to the Greek belief that the winds fertilize the sacred waters or the case of the mother of Buddha who was also a virgin; Zeus begetting Athena alone, the father producing without copulation; the golden egg of Brahma giving birth to the seven Rishis in a manner similar to the way the lotus flower made the Egyptian god Ra appear; Zeus fertilizing Danae with golden rain (urine).

2. Birth: the legend of Jonah vomited by the whale; Little Red Riding Hood devoured by the wolf and reborn by laparotomy; Leda's egg which was like Brahma's; the queen who ate a monkey's excrement for butter and evacuated little monkeys.

3. The Oedipus complex: Cronus who castrates the father of Uranus and later out of fear of his own sons devours them one by one, except the last one, Zeus, who conquers and dethrones him; Osiris who was castrated as was Pelops; Snow White and her stepmother, the diabolical image of the "bad mother;" Cinderella and her stepmother; Tom Thumb and the Cat with the Seven League Boots, perfectly associated with the phallus according to dream analysis.

Pôrto-Carrero also proposed a classification tied to natural phenomena. It contradicts the theory that certain myths and legends are derived from the interpretation of nature. For Pôrto-Carrero they rather take on the role of sexual symbols and follow the same process of development as infantile fantasies. In this way "The Deserted Village of the Moon" and "How Night Was Born" are indigenous legends filled with sex symbols. The first is a proved expression of incestuous crime, while in the second the maternal belly is symbolized by a tucuma palm's core and the phallus by a large snake and by fire. In this legend a number of serfs open a sacred urn from which emerges the night, a favorable time for lovers. In other words, a deflowering takes place.

ÉDISON CARNEIRO: DIALECTICAL MATERIALISM

Among the criticism of psychoanalytical folklore are those based on dialectical and historical materialism. In Brazil, Édison Carneiro is the foremost exponent of this position. Although his contributions should properly be studied in a work dealing with the relationship between folklore and materialism, it is not amiss to consider them here.

Carneiro once studied under Ramos but soon completely separated himself in matters dealing with analytical demopsychology. Perhaps even psychoanalysis has no value for Carneiro and on this he is one with Luriia, Vnukov, Veidemiuller, Kolbanovskii, and others mentioned by Joseph Wortis (69:89–96).

An example of his disagreement with Ramos is typified by the following events which occurred in 1937 soon after he began his career. It concerns the "Last Will of the Ox." Ramos felt that it was a "totemic meal" in which "the children seek redemption for the crime committed against the father, or at least symbolic communion with the *Urvater*." On the other hand, Carneiro felt that it was unquestionably an expression of the "evolution of the productive forces of society" (10:176). Following this theme, he wrote *Dinâmica do folclore*, a short and not very mature essay, which for the first time submits folklore in Brazil to the treatment of dialectical and historical materialism.

From this point of view, folklore acquires a feeling of "social claim," the characteristics of a weapon—albeit a rudimentary one— against the class interests in the bourgeois state as defined by the Marxists. In this Carneiro is in complete agreement with Sokolov, Gorky, and others. The "burning of Judas," the "bate-pau dance," the "Capoeira," the "Bumba-meu-boi," the "Congadas," and the other examples of popular entertainment would thus be fundamentally loud protests against universal social injustice, claims for the "right to work, peace, civil liberty, economic well-being, and happiness on earth" (9:9–34).

ROGER BASTIDE: PSYCHOANALYTICAL SOCIOLOGY

Roger Bastide is worth noting in the history of psychoanalytical folklore, although he rightfully belongs among psychoanalytical sociologists. In any case his *Sociologia e Psicandlise* (4) relates to folklore. As a parallel to Ramos in Brazilian folklore, Bastide is the sociological psychoanalyst of general sociology in Brazil. He systematized psychoanalytical sociology without, however, citing examples from Brazilian life. Ramos did the exact opposite. Without ever writing a general treatise on folklore and psychoanalysis he filled his work on the Brazilian Negro with examples of analytical demopsychology. Ramos was the most perfect psychoanalytical folklorist of Brazilian folklore but never of general folklore.

Bastide is of interest to the psychoanalytical folklorist because of his observations on the following topics: the libido, the castration complex, censure, symbolism, sublimation, and the principle of reality. The same is true of his statements on the relations of myths and dreams, the collective unconscious, psychoanalytical criminology, and psychoanalysis and Marxism. In his criticism of Freud's psychoanalysis, Bastide analyzes extensively the reactions of other sociologists and anthropologists.

He cites examples on very few occasions and frequently only identifies the type of sociology. In other words he provides abstract examples as follows: (a) sociology of the oral libido—nourishment, cannibalism; (b) sociology of the anal libido—excrement in magic, medicine, and primitive rituals; (c) sociology of narcissim—magic, taboo, avoidances, animism, religion; (d) general libido—clothing, fire, initiation rites; and (e) sociology of the trauma of birth—the dwelling. Within the general libido are the totemic exegesis of music and the ritual ceremonies of sacrifice. These are followed by pages on the psychoanalysis of language, the plastic arts, and the family.

BERNARDO CANAL-FEIJOO: FOLKLORE IN ARGENTINA

In Bernardo Canal-Feijoo's interesting study *Burla, credo, culpa en la creación anónima (sociología, etnología y psicología en el folklore)* he attempted to focus attention on the folkloric state of being. This is a problem which is not always considered in studies dealing with folklore. What are the interior forces which help it to develop and on which it subsists? (7:254).

To answer this question he analyzed different folkloric species and stated that the inner force of fables was mockery, as explained by sociologists; that of worship and feasts was faith, as clarified by ethnologists; and that of the legend is guilt, as researched by psychologists. As concrete examples, he referred to the fables about the fox and the legends of the "Kakuy" and the "Widow."*

It is obvious that the chapter of interest to psychoanalytical folklorists is the one concerning guilt. I must emphasize, however, that the latter does not fall exclusively in the province of the legend as one may gather when reading Canal-Feijoo. There are in fact no special reasons why the Oedipus complex cannot be perceived also in other folkloric species in the same geographical region— fables as well as worship and feasts. I will verify this in my case studies. I believe that Canal-Feijoo is of the same opinion although he limited himself to the legend-guilt binomial.

Without a doubt his contribution is a pioneer one in Argentina. I could criticize his organization, or even the anarchy in his bibliographical references, or the erudite character of his examples, but I believe that in the future he will be duly recognized in the folkloric movement in his own country. He will stand out when the time and place of his studies are considered. We must not forget that these psychoanalytical comments on the legend and fable were included in essays in 1938 and 1940, in his works *Mitos perdidos* and *Los Casos de Juan*, when no one in Argentina had yet considered these topics. *Burla, credo, culpa en la creación anonima* is nothing more than an augmented and improved edition of those first works, written thirteen years later.

MARIE LANGER: CULTURALIST OF MODERN PSYCHOANALYSIS

Marie Langer starts with culture, as do Kardiner and Mead, to explain dreams and lunacy, among other phenomena. Thus if one knew the folklore of an area, one would know the types of dreams of its inhabitants as well as their types of insanity. To prove this thesis she took a concrete object, the folkloric picture of the Evil

*"Kakuy" is a Quechua term; "urutaú" is used in Guarani.

Mother,* and compared it with the oneiric image and the lunatic image. According to the frequency with which this image appears in folklore it also appears in these other media.

Marie Langer's contribution to Latin American analytical demopsychology consists in having called the attention of her psychoanalyst colleagues to anthropology as a result of her noteworthy study *Maternidad y sexo* (1951).

To illustrate her point she cites the following dream of one of her clients, a young lesbian:

> She sees a tree and in its shade a number of piglets. Looking more closely, she discovers an enormous spider-crab suspended from the tree. The spider immediately begins to come down. The piglets run away with the exception of one who stays as if fascinated and paralyzed. The spider falls on top of it and begins to suck its blood. The sleeper, horrified, sees that the poor piglet is unsuccessful in defending itself and the pink color of its skin becomes pale and white because the spider has sucked out all its blood.

And she interprets it this way:

> I can accelerate the interpretation of this dream about the three little pigs—known as three brothers in Walt Disney's comics—by stating that they represent the dreamer's two younger sisters. The spider, as usually happens in dreams and folkloric material, symbolizes the mother (46:100).

She continues by correlating it with the following pathological case which also occurred under the influence of the Evil Mother:

> A young married couple hires a servant since the wife is pregnant and almost due. The baby is born. A few weeks later the husband and wife go to the movies one evening, leaving the baby in the servant's care. Until that time she has always been reliable. According to one version, on their return she receives them ceremoniously dressed in the wife's bridal gown and tells them she has prepared quite a surprise for them. She bids them come into the dining room to serve them a special meal. They enter and find a horrifying spectacle. In the middle of the table, placed there with great care, they see their son on a large platter, roasted and garnished with

---

*As we shall see, the Evil Mother is the son's image of the mother resulting from the castration complex.

44

potatoes. The poor mother goes insane at once. She loses her speech and no one has heard her utter a single word since then. The father, according to several versions, is a military man. He pulls out a revolver and shoots the servant. Then he runs away and is never heard from again (46:98–99).

She compares it to the stories of Snow White and Hansel and Gretel, in which the Evil Mother is very much in evidence, and personified in the classic character of "sorceress" or "old witch."

As will have been noted we are far from having exhausted the roster of authors dealing with psychoanalytical folklore. I wished merely to present a sample to which must be added such names as Patrick Mullahy, Marie Bonaparte, Mircea Eliade, Richard Thurnwald, and E. Harding. Ernest Jones' statement should not be forgotten: "An immense amount of psychoanalytical work has been published on these fascinating subjects" (40:96).

Part Two: Theory

3

Metapsychology

The short history just presented on analytical demopsychology or psychoanalytical folklore—terms selected to identify folklore and its relationship to psychoanalysis—shows us the way to develop the theory of psychoanalysis. This chapter is also a chapter of history but with one difference: it does not start with a chronological listing of scholars but focuses rather on some of their studies. We will deal with orthodox and heterodox aspects of psychoanalytical theory of paramount interest to folklore, both in this section on metapsychology and in the one on the collective unconscious in the following chapter. Subsequent chapters contain concrete examples which are interpreted according to these theories. In this presentation I will, of course, confine myself to a didactic order appropriate to the discipline. The hierarchic prerogatives of these theories are treated less prominently.

It is the opinion of Edward Glover, an enthusiastic Freudian, that Freud includes the study of mental structure, the energies which make this mental structure function, and its observed mechanism for the control of these energies under the term metapsychology. This tripartite focus makes up Freudian metapsychology. Although we lack elements for its proof—since it appears to me that under the rubric of metapsychology Freud includes only the study of the psychic mechanism—we will accept Glover's statement. Our metapsychological analysis is therefore divided into three aspects: mental structure, mental energy, and mental mechanism.

For greater clarity we quote the following explanation from Glover: "The description of mental processes involves a threefold approach to the subject. Although the psychologist is not concerned with the locality of mind, he finds himself compelled to postulate for purposes of presentation a certain degree of mental organization which can be conveniently referred to as mental *structure*. Having done so he is then compelled to describe the *energies* which activate this organization or apparatus. Once embarked on this process he cannot stop short of describing the *mechanisms* by which the mental apparatus regulates these energies. This threefold approach constitutes what Freud termed the metapsychological approach to the descriptive data, either reported or introspected, that constitute the raw material of psychology" (37:21).

MENTAL ENERGY

For the exploration of some of the principal tenets of basic psychological theory, we could use secondary sources. Although this would have been adequate years ago, the student now has available the excellent translation of Freud's *Complete Works* by James Strachey. Furthermore, direct contact with Freud's works will work toward the elimination of certain prejudices against his ideas which still exist. These have resulted from confused criticism, the mundane snobbism of our time, and the backward and antisocial conservatism of certain religious organizations. At times we run into prejudices of a sexual nature which appear in conversations preceded by the statement, "I do not like these essays."

The libido is Freud's basic contribution to the study of human sexual behavior. It is discussed principally in *Three Essays on the Theory of Sexuality* (1905), *The Infant's Genital Organization* (1907–1923), *Five Lectures on Psychoanalysis* (1910), "On Narcissism: An Introduction" (1914), and *Introduction to Psychoanalysis* (1916–1918).

The libido is described over and over again in different contexts and from different points of view. For example: "The fact of the existence of sexual needs in human beings and animals is expressed in biology by the assumption of a 'sexual instinct,' or the analogy of the instinct of nutrition, that is, of hunger. Everyday language possesses no counterpart to the word 'hunger,' but science makes use of the word 'libido' for that purpose" (33:21). In other words, "We find in children at a very early age manifestations of those instinctual components of sexual pleasure (or, as we like to say, of libido)" (25:44). The libido is a term then which designates the dynamic manifestations of sexuality, and it was first used in psychoanalysis by Freud.

A clearer understanding of libido is to be had from the study of its development. Let us study it, but not before knowing what is a sexual object and what is a sexual aim. By sexual object Freud means "the person from whom sexual attraction proceeds," and "the act toward which the instinct tends the sexual aim" (33:22). His outstanding essay on "Sexual Aberrations" stems from this distinction between sexual object and sexual aim, and in it he studies deviations relative to the object (impuberals and animals as sexual objects and perverts) and deviations relative to the sexual aims (sexual use of the mucous tissue of the mouth and lips, use of the anal orifice, and fetishism). Concerning this I also suggest *Psychoanalytical Method and the Doctrine of Freud* by Dalbiez, a work which has an excellent didactic design (21).

The development of the libido, tied to the sexual object and aim, conditions the appearance of the three sexual phases of human behavior: the oral, the anal, and the genital. The latter, corresponding to the behavior of adults and coming after puberty, had already been explored. The rest was not known. Most of the scientists of the past century never suspected the existence of an infantile sexuality. Nothing else belonged in the area of sexual behavior than those acts related to reproduction. The astonishment in scientific circles produced by Freud's work can well be imagined when he wrote about and defended the presence of sexual behavior from the very beginning of the post-uterine life of man. Freud wrote, ". . . it is certainly not the case that the sexual instinct enters into children at the age of puberty in the way in which, in the Gospel, the devil entered into the swine. A child has its sexual instincts and activities from the first; it comes into the world with them; and, after an important course of development passing through many stages, they lead to what is known as the normal sexuality of the adult. There is even no difficulty in observing the manifestations of these sexual activities in children;

on the contrary, it calls for some skill to overlook them or explain them away" (25:42).

Freud described these different phases of the libido many times, on occasion going into minute detail, and on others synthesizing to the utmost, as in the following example: "A child's sexual instinct turns out to be put together out of a number of factors; it is capable of being divided up into numerous components which originate from various sources. Above all, it is still independent of the reproductive function, into the service of which it will later be brought. It serves for the acquisition of different kinds of pleasurable feeling, which, basing ourselves on analogies and connections, we bring together under the idea of sexual pleasure. The chief source of infantile sexual pleasure is the appropriate excitation of certain parts of the body that are especially susceptible to stimulus: apart from the genitals, these are the oral, anal and urethral orifices, as well as the skin and other sensory surfaces. . . . We call the parts of the body that are important in the acquisition of sexual pleasure 'erotogenic zones'. Thumb-sucking (or sensual sucking) in the youngest infants is a good example of this auto-erotic satisfaction from an erotogenic zone. The first scientific observer of this phenomenon, a paediatrician in Budapest named Lindner (1879), already interpreted it correctly as sexual satisfaction and described exhaustively its transition to other and higher forms of sexual activity. . . . These instincts occur in pairs of opposites, active and passive. I may mention as the most important representatives of this group the desire to cause pain (sadism) with its passive counterpart (masochism) and the active and passive desire for looking, from the former of which curiosity branches off later on and from the latter the impulsion to artistic and theatrical display. Others of a child's sexual activities already imply the making of an 'object-choice', where an extraneous person becomes the main feature, a person who owes his importance in the first instance to considerations arising from the self-preservative instinct. But at this early period of childhood difference in sex plays no decisive part as yet. Thus you can attribute some degree of homosexuality to every child without doing him an injustice. This widespread and copious but dissociated sexual life of children, in which each separate instinct pursues its own acquisition of pleasure independently of all the rest, is now brought together and organized in two main directions, so that by the end of puberty the individual's final sexual character is as a rule completely formed. On the one hand, the separate instincts become subordinated to the dominance of the genital zone, so that the whole sexual life enters the service of reproduction, and the satisfaction of the separate instincts retains its importance only as preparing for and encouraging the sexual act proper. On the other hand, object-choice pushes auto-erotism into the background, so that in the subject's erotic life all the components of the sexual instinct now seek satisfaction in relation to the person who is loved. Not all of the original sexual components, however, are admitted to take part in this final establishment of sexuality. Even before puberty extremely energetic repressions of certain instincts have been effected under the influence of education, and mental forces such as shame, disgust and morality have been set up, which, like watchmen, maintain these repressions. So that when at puberty the high tide of sexual demands is reached, it is met by these mental reactive or resistant structures like dams, which direct its flow into what are called normal channels and make it impossible for it to reactivate the instincts that have undergone repression" (25:43–45). His detailed descriptions, of course, teach us a great deal more. We can perceive the process of partial libido formation through them and understand the relationships which bring them together.

We thus see that the child's first important need, to satiate his hunger, changes his mouth, because of the permanent excitation of food, into a region of high erogenic response. Freud states that "We apply to that activity of a given bodily area which consists in conveying sexually exciting stimuli to the mind the term *erotogenicity*" (31:41). The child soon separates the need for food from the pure pleasure of sucking. Sucking develops from suckling. Sucking is the free fulfillment of the libido. The child sucks the pacifier, his thumb, and even his big toes. This is said to be a frankly autoerotic activity since the child does not suck the thumb nor any other part of anyone except himself. The object of the libido is found in himself. The oral libido is a purely autoerotic libido.

Weaning and the development of teeth soon occur, and the act of chewing more frequently begins to displace suckling. Furthermore, there is an intensification of social coercion. Social behavior restrains infantile preferences for sucking, taking away his pacifier and repeating several times a day, "How dirty!" and expressions like that, in addition to spanking him. These social coercions develop reproaches in him. And this reproach with all its train of esthetic and ethical ideas which are just beginning to form (modesty, fear, loathing) creates repressions. Sucking is abandoned and the child desperately seeks other avenues for the fulfillment of his libido. He finds these in the anus.

The continued irritation of the anal orifice by the passage of excrement awakens the erogeneity lacking in the anus or which was already there but temporarily exceeded by the mouth's erogeneity. The child's entire interest now turns to the anus and its substitutes. The feces acquire symbolic meanings. The child esteems them, loves them, plays with them. He prefers to deposit them in his pants rather than in the toilet, since they are a part of himself. As parts of himself he feels it just to offer them to his mother. They thus acquire the meaning of a gift to his mother, a gift prepared with profound pleasure. On the other hand, there is great pleasure in retaining them, a pleasure equal to that of sucking in the past.

But the mother understands nothing about this gift. It becomes a difficult task to clean him as well as the sheets or the floor here and there. Because of this, the pressure of social coercion is unremitting.

A whole chaotic world of orders and counterorders faces the child. He respected the orders to stop sucking. And "they" now follow him in his new beloved games. If not from the mouth, if not from the anus, where then will he derive the satisfaction needed for these mysterious forces? Of course it is his subconscious "reasoning" which follows this line. Reproach, on the other hand, bothers him. The weight of the struggle overwhelms him. The exploitation of the anus as a source of pleasure takes place then far removed from the eyes of parents and other adults. Bound by the same fate, persecuted and misunderstood, children share this misfortune. A gregarious sentiment brings them together. "Prohibited games" take place where the active is not essentially different from the passive.

At this time a sensational discovery makes a profound impression on their minds and it will have deep consequences: the differences between sexes. The irritation of the genitals by the act of urinating, and even the organic development of the genitals, now take the child's attention completely away from his former erotogenic zones. The genitals become the primary erotogenic region and autoeroticism finds support in masturbation. Narcissism alternates with sustained attempts to find the sexual object outside of his own body.

Social coercion accelerates this search. The adolescent eventually projects himself in another being—objective, genital libido. Conquering the Oedipus complex, he selects someone similar to the image of his mother. This does not happen without many conflicts, wandering down dark paths filled with unforseen dangers.

Narcissism

Narcissism and the Oedipus complex are derived from the two autoerotic and pregenital phases—oral libido and anal libido—and are among several manifestations of the normal development of the libido. These manifestations also have a close relationship with folklore.

Narcissism originates specifically with sucking. On having recourse to autoeroticism, the child tends to exaggerate it for succeedingly greater pleasurable consequences each time. The child is sufficient for himself and is thankful that he is able to satisfy himself. This thankfulness redounds in the ego's hyperesteem, which is what constitutes narcissism. "The word narcissism," Freud writes in his "On Narcissism: An Introduction," is taken from clinical terminology, and was chosen by P. Nacke in 1899 to denote the attitude of a person who treats his own body in the same way as otherwise the body of a sexual object is treated; that is to say, he experiences sexual pleasure in gazing at, caressing, and fondling his body, till complete gratification ensues upon these activities" (31:30). "This narcissistic organization is never wholly abandoned," Freud states in his *Totem and Taboo*. "A human being remains to some extent narcissistic even after he has found external objects for his libido" (34:89).

The Oedipus Complex

The Oedipus complex, on the other hand, is the first sign of reaction against autoeroticism. It appears just as the child tends to exteriorize the projection of his libido. Obliged to stop sucking, he then seeks an object foreign to him. Carried away by memories, such as those of nursing, he tends to select the mother. According to Freud it is selection by apposition (31:47). But social coercion, among other factors, forces him to continue being autoerotic, with his libido moved from the region of the mouth to the anal region. While the Oedipus complex survives, the child is autoerotic and very strongly narcissistic.

Let us try to go deeper into this important and fundamental complex. Its consequences are so extensive in adult behavior that it is even considered the basic complex of psychoanalysis. Let us begin by recapitulating with Freud. We have seen that the mother's breast is the first object of the mouth during the development of the libido. It satisfies the child's need for nourishment. The erotic element satisfied by the mother's breast, overcomes his independence by sucking, an action which allows him to separate himself from a foreign object and replace it by part of the child's own body. The tendency of the oral region then becomes autoerotic as are the anal and other erotogenic tendencies from the beginning (26).

Freud indicates that subsequent development pursues two objectives: first, the giving up of autoeroticism, that is, replacing the object which is part of the individual's own body by one which is foreign to it and outside of it; and second, the union of the different objects and replace them by one object only. The finding of the first exterior object is the final process of the autoerotic infantile cycle of sucking. Says Freud: "It may be emphasized that, when the process has reached a certain point in the years of childhood before the latency period, the object adopted proves almost identical with the first object of the oral pleasure impulse, adopted by reason of the child's dependent relationship to it; that is, namely, the mother, although not the mother's breast. We call the mother the first love-object. We speak of 'love' when we lay accent upon the mental side of the sexual impulses and disregard, or wish to forget for a moment, the demands of the fundamental physical or 'sensual' side of the impulses. At about the time when the mother becomes the love-object, the mental operation of repression has already begun in the child and has withdrawn from him the knowledge of some part of his sexual aims" (25:338–339).

The coercion of the exterior social world on the child—attempting to make it understand the impossibility of these inconsequential aspirations being realized—coincides with the love of the mother. The mother becomes unattainable. She is sacred and prohibited, taboo. This ambivalence of sentiments (prohibited desire) is accompanied by feelings of hostility against the outside world. And this hostile and dreadful exterior world is represented for the child in the first instance by the father, for obvious reasons: the mother does not inspire that ambivalence which constrains the child. The father then is a competitor, a rival. The child feels that the father is stealing from him the caresses from his mother which are his due. He must be hated, killed. And this death and hatred function symbolically like a sage defense of the organism, releasing it from nervous tension and freeing it from certain neuroses. It is a struggle between two opposing forces: love of mother, and his own psychic efforts at repression and prohibition which develop primarily as a result of social pressure. Freud labeled this struggle the Oedipus complex. As long as the child does not successfully avoid the Oedipus complex, the family drama continues. The child must find a way out of this conflict by himself. Satisfying himself with the mother is not possible. Killing his father, his greatest enemy, is not easy.

The solution may be a relative stilling of his desires. It is a calming down which characterizes the latency period, from approximately five years of age to the emergence of puberty. It is during puberty that the genitals begin their epic as the most effective erogenous zone. Organic sexual development reaches its highest peak. Consequently the individual returns to the search of an object. Motivated by his recollections he seeks out the mother yet one time more. That is to say, he revives the Oedipus complex once more. But the individual soon finds a positive solution, a way to definitely escape from it. And this solution rests on the satisfactory location of another "mother" on which paternal prohibitions do not devolve. It is the only compensation which resolves the problem normally. The Oedipus complex, of nostalgic memory, is filed away in the subconscious. Those who do not know how to endure it or to escape from it fall into neuroses. Only psychoanalytical therapy, providing us with a picture of ourselves, will effect a cure. What we have just said in our own words we can read here and there in Freud in his many works. The following excerpts have been selected as examples:

"The child's first choice of an object, which derives from its need for help, claims our further interest. Its choice is directed in the first instance to all those who look after it, but these soon give place to its parents. Children's relations to their parents, as we learn alike from direct observations of children and from later analytic examination of adults, are by no means free from elements of accompanying sexual excitation. The child takes both of its parents, and more particularly one of them, as the object of its erotic wishes. In so doing, it usually follows some indication from its parents, whose affection bears the clearest characteristics of sexual activity, even though of one that is inhibited in its aims. As a rule a father prefers his daughter and a mother her son; the child reacts to this by wishing, if he is a son, to take his father's place, and, if she is a daughter, her mother's. The feelings which are aroused in these relations between parents and children and in the resulting ones between brothers and sisters are not only of a positive or affectionate kind but also of a negative or hostile one. The complex which is thus formed is doomed to early repression; but it continues to exercise a great and lasting influence from the unconscious. It is to be suspected that, together with its extensions, it constitutes the *nuclear complex* of every neurosis, and we may expect to find it no less actively at work in other regions of mental life" (25:47).

"The clinical fact which confronts us behind the form of the Oedipus complex as established by analysis now becomes of the greatest practical importance. We learn that at the time of puberty, when the sexual instinct first asserts its demands in full strength, the old familiar incestuous objects are taken up again and again invested by the libido. The infantile object-choice was but a feeble venture in play, as it were, but it laid down the direction for the object-choice of puberty. At this time a very intense flow of feeling towards the Oedipus complex or in reaction to it comes into force; since their mental antecedents have become intolerable, however, these feelings must remain for the most part outside consciousness. From the time of puberty onward the human individual must devote himself to the great task of *freeing himself from the parents;* and only after this detachment is accomplished can he cease to be a child and so become a member of the social community. For a son, the task consists in releasing his libidinal desires from his mother, in order to employ them in the quest of an external love-object in reality; and in reconciling himself with his father if he has remained antagonistic to him, or in freeing himself from his domination if, in the reaction to the infantile revolt, he has lapsed into subservience to him. These tasks are laid down for every man; it is noteworthy how seldom they are carried through ideally, that is, how seldom they are solved in a manner psychologically as well as socially satisfactory. In neurotics, however, this detachment from the parents is not accomplished at all; the son remains all his life in subjection to his father, and incapable of transferring his libido to a new sexual object. In the reversed relationship the daughter's fate may be the same. In this sense the Oedipus complex is justifiably regarded as the kernel of the neuroses" (26:345–346).

"The processes at puberty thus establish the primacy of the genital zones; and in a man, the penis, which has now become capable of erection, presses foward insistently towards the new sexual aim—penetration into a cavity in the body which excites his genital zone. Simultaneously, on the psychical side the process of finding an object, for which preparations have been made from earliest childhood, is completed. At a time at which the first beginnings of sexual satisfaction are still linked with the taking of nourishment, the sexual instinct has a sexual object outside the infant's own body in the shape of his mother's breast. It is only later that the instinct loses that object, just at the time, perhaps, when the child is able to form a total idea of the person to whom the organ that is giving satisfaction belongs. As a rule the sexual instinct then becomes auto-erotic, and not until the period of latency has been passed through is the original relation restored. There are thus good reasons why a child sucking at his mother's breast has become the prototype of every relation of love. The finding of an object is in fact a refinding of it" (33:124–125).

We could quote quite a bit more from Freud. But let us not forget from what has been stated that the Oedipus complex passes through three phases: conflict, latency, and resurrection. Furthermore, "identification" precedes them and follows in step with them and because of this we gave it special attention.

We believe it unnecessary at this time to make the Oedipus complex valid also for the daughter. The frame of reference is almost the same, but in reverse. The amorous objective of the daughter is the father, the honey of her sexual dreams, an object which is sacred and prohibited at the same time. The power which punishes and represses is the mother, the terrible mother who steals the affection of the father from the daughter. We can call it the "Electra complex." We believe it therefore unnecessary to recount the legend which gave its name to this complex which has already been analyzed by Freud in his *Introduction to Psychoanalysis*. (26:339) For those who wish to study Sophocles' *Oedipus Rex* in depth we recommend the version in Patrick Mullahy's study, *Oedipus, Myth and Complex* (52).

Identification

Identification is part of the prehistory of the Oedipus complex, according to Freud's point of view. We cannot, however, consider it solely as a phase of the Oedipus complex since it functions independently also. As a result of this mechanism of affective relationship of a primary nature, the child seeks to escape from auto-eroticism by attempting to find a new object for his libido outside of himself. Identification, then precedes selection. Before selecting the mother, the child identifies with her, the father, or loved ones.

Freud believes that identification in psychoanalysis means the earliest manifestation of an affective relationship with another person. Consequently the child manifests a special interest for his father. He would like to be like him and replace him in everything. His father thus becomes his ideal. This conduct absolutely does not represent a passive attitude or a feminine one toward the father (or man in general) but rather it is strictly masculine and reconciles itself well with the Oedipus complex to the development of which it contributes. Simultaneous to this identification with the father, or somewhat later, the child begins to adopt his mother as the object of his libidinous instincts. This shows then two types of relationships that are psychologically different. The mother is frankly a sexual object, while the father is a model to be imitated. These two relationships coexist for a while without influencing or hampering each other. But since psychic behavior tends toward unification, they come closer to each other until they finally meet, and from this confluence the normal Oedipus complex is born. The child perceives the father as barring the way to the mother, and because of this his identification with the father acquires a hostility which becomes the desire to substitute for him where the mother is concerned.

In the same chapter Freud adds, "Identification, in fact, is ambivalent from the very first; it can turn into an expression of tenderness as easily as into a wish for someone's removal. It behaves like a derivative of the first, *oral* phase of the organization of the libido, in which the object that we long for and prize is assimilated by eating and is in that way annihilated as such. The cannibal, as we know, has remained at this standpoint; he has a devouring affection for his enemies and only devours people of whom he is fond" (27:105). "Identification," and the "selection of an object" are therefore distinct phenomena. One is what one would like to be, the other is what one would like to have, according to Freud.

This distinction facilitates comprehension of the genesis of many neurotic symptoms, even including sexual perversion. These phenomena result when identification has taken the place of selection. Breaking down this formula Freud writes, "A young man has been unusually long and intensely fixated upon his mother in the sense of the Oedipus complex. But at last, after the end of puberty, the time comes for exchanging his mother for some other sexual object. Things take a sudden turn: the young man does not abandon his mother, but identifies himself with her; he transforms himself into her, and now looks about for objects which can replace his ego for him, and on which he can bestow such love and care as he has experienced from his mother. This is a frequent process, which can be confirmed as often as one likes, and which is naturally quite independent from any hypothesis that may be made as to the organic driving force and the motives of the sudden transformation" (27:108).

The fact that Freud has not dealt in great detail with identification in his essays on sexual theory is brought to mind. He should have dealt with it here. He does so only in *Group Psychology* (1921) concerning primitive forms of affective relationships. With this then we are on the way to considering "identification" as one of the ultimate Freudian concepts. In folklore, as we shall see, it is a common phenomenon.

Infantile Sexual Curiosity

Between the ages of three and five, in the midst of the Oedipus complex phase there develops in the child what Freud calls the instinct for knowledge (*Wisstrieb*) or instinct for research. They are the endless years of questions. And these questions are preferentially on sexual themes.

The child wishes to unmask the enigma of birth, and generally that of his little brother (the enigma of the Sphinx), fearful of losing the attention of those who surround him. He then builds a whole series of fantasies surrounding birth. The tale of the stork which his parents tell him does not really succeed in convincing him. According to Freud he develops the strangest anatomical solutions. "Children come out of the breast," or "they are taken out by cutting the mother's body," or "they come out by opening a way through the navel," or even, "they are born by coming out of the intestines like the act of passing excrement." Freud indicates that this research in the child's early years is rarely remembered outside of the analysis, since it is subdued by controls. It results when successfully brought to mind, revealing a complete and intimate analogy (33:92–95).

Soon, halfway through his investigation, as we have already stated, the child makes a sensational discovery. He discovers that not everyone whom he knows has a genital organ like his own. Between maintaining his former belief in the equality of the sexes, or succumbing to factual evidence, one more new complex is established in the child, one of grave impact: the castration complex. Under the influence of this complex the child orients a large part of his attention to the male organ itself. The paternal reaction to the special care the child gives his organ, in general, aggravates the castration complex, and threatens the poor child with the amputation of the penis.

The same sensational discovery by the girl is clothed in a different aspect. In the girl the castration complex is characterized by jealousy of the penis and a desire to possess it inside her. Freud states that the girl succumbs to jealousy of the penis, and this jealousy culminates in the desire—which is very important because of its consequences—to be a boy. The future of the girl, on becoming a woman, depends a great deal on how she has succeeded in overcoming the castration complex. It may well not be overcome and the woman does not then reach the perfection of femininity expected of her. Neuroses and perversions (masculine women, for example) can be seen daily as survivals and traumas of the castration complex in its first childhood appearance. The solution is found in transfer. Envy of the penis must be substituted for the desire of possessing the man, even though he is an indispensable accessory for the penis. Later the desire to have male children develops, as a compensation for masculinity, although the penis which is produced belongs to the son. It is especially important to recall the following quotations from Freud concerning this matter:

"Infantile sexual curiosity begins very early, sometimes before the third year. It is not connected with the difference between the sexes, which is nothing to children, since they—the boys, at least— ascribe the same male genital organ to both sexes. If then a boy discovers the vagina in a little sister or playmate, he at once tries to deny the evidence of his senses; for he cannot conceive of a human being like himself without his most important attribute. Later, he is horrified at the possibilities it reveals to him; the influence of previous threats occasioned by too great a preoccupation with his own little member now begins to be felt. He comes under the dominion of the castration complex, which will play such a large part in the formation of his character if he remains healthy, and of his neurosis if he falls ill, and of his resistance if he comes under analytic treatment. Of little girls we know that they feel themselves heavily handicapped by the absence of a large visible penis and envy the boy's possession of it; from this source primarily springs the wish to be a man which is resumed again later in the neurosis, owing to some maladjustment to female development. The clitoris in the girl, moreover, is in every way equivalent during childhood to the penis; it is a region of special excitability in which autoerotic satisfaction is achieved" (26:326–327).

"The sexual researches of these early years of childhood are always carried out in solitude. They constitute a first step towards taking an independent attitude in the world, and imply a high degree of alienation of the child from the people in his environment who formerly enjoyed his complete confidence" (33:94–95).

The phenomena related to the libido do not end with the castration complex. At least two are essential for an understanding of analytical demopsychology: anxiety and symbolism.

Anxiety

Anxiety is an affective state. Freud studied it under this concept in various works, especially in his *Inhibitions, Symptoms and*

Anxiety and *New Introductory Lectures to Psychoanalysis* (28:77–174; 30:81–111). As he understood it, anxiety is an affective state characterized by an unpleasantness. But this unpleasantness is very special and can be distinguished from other unpleasant sensations such as anguish, pain, and sadness.

To complete the task of defining anxiety Freud had recourse to Rank's famous *The Trauma of Birth*. Rank saw the genesis of anxiety specifically in the trauma of birth, a phenomenon he used to label his study. According to him, anxiety is the consequence of the unconscious memory of this trauma. Freud, on the other hand, felt that it was not the recollection of a happy intrauterine existence but rather the result of the warning of a state of "danger," characterized in general by "dissatisfaction," that is, the "development of the pressure of need." The child consequently takes note of this state of danger when he feels dissatisfied and only feels satisfied when the pressure of necessity is overcome. The necessity in turn makes itself felt with the loss of an object.

Thus some fundamental cases of the childist manifestation of anxiety are understandable. Freud states that anxiety is present when the child is alone, when he finds himself in the dark, and when he meets a strange person instead of a familiar one. Furthermore, these three situations are reduced to one condition alone, that of noticing the need for the loved one. Anxiety develops thus as a reaction to noticing the lack of the object.

Other situations exist similar to these. The castration complex is a limitless generator of anxiety since it implies the idea of loss. Freud develops many other considerations including the fact that anxiety is developed exclusively in the ego and never in the superego or the id. This explains the different intensities of anxiety in accordance with the ego's development.

Symbolism

Symbolism is a resource of the libido by which it unburdens itself when it is impossible to do so directly. It is very difficult to understand since it requires prior knowledge of the libido and the structures and mechanisms of the psyche.

Transcending psychoanalysis, its study will also depend on other disciplines, folklore in particular. It was here that Freud located the basis for the relations between psychoanalysis and folklore. The same symbols expressed in dreams and by the unconscious while awake appear many times in folkloric pieces. He indicated that we must observe that this symbolism does not belong to dreams exclusively but it is a characteristic representation of the unconscious, especially that of the general populace. It is revealed to us in folklore, myths, fables, idiomatic expressions, proverbs, and common jokes of the people, much more fully and completely than in dreams. Consequently to give the symbol all the attention merited by its importance, and to discuss the many problems inherent in the concept—problems which are largely unsolved— would require us to exceed to a considerable extent the topic of oneiric interpretation.

Freud even went so far as to take up an entire page analyzing symbols in folkloric pieces. He did so in 1916 when his *A General Introduction to Psychoanalysis* summarized his *Interpretation of Dreams* (1901). Here he again stated that he owed his concept of symbolism not only to oneiric observation but also to folklore. You will ask: "Do I then really live in the midst of sexual symbols? Are all the objects around me, all the clothes I wear, all the things I handle, always sexual symbols and nothing else?" There is really good reason for surprised questions, and the first of these would be: "How do we profess to arrive at the meaning of these dream symbols, about which the dreamer himself can give us little or no information?"

Freud replies: "My answer is that we derive our knowledge from widely different sources: from fairy tales and myths, jokes and witticisms, and from folklore, that is, from what we know of the manners and customs, sayings and songs, of different peoples, and from poetic and colloquial usage of language. Everywhere in these various fields the same symbolism occurs, and in many of them we can understand it without being taught anything about it. If we consider these various sources individually, we shall find so many parallels to dream symbolism that we are bound to be convinced of the correctness of our interpretations" (26:166).

On concluding his folkloric psychoanalytical essay Freud examines amulets and popular sayings, and points out how much a specialist instead of an amateur like himself could achieve in this field: "You can imagine how much richer and more interesting a collection of this sort might be made, not by dilettanti like ourselves, but by real experts in mythology, anthropology, philosophy, and folklore. We are forced to certain conclusions, which cannot be exhaustive, but nevertheless will give us plenty to think about" (26:173).

But let us look at the concept of the symbol, a concept which has been developed from the study of the component parts of dreams. Freud observed two kinds of content in dreams which he called respectively manifested content and latent content. The former is the oneiric configuration as it occurs under the influence of libidinous energy. The latter is the true meaning of the dream which only becomes clear through analysis. Censure is relaxed in the oneiric process and the unconscious material can emerge without difficulty. But it is not all released and because of this situations arise in which the oneiric material is displaced and thus disguised. The disguise is primarily effected through symbols.

The symbol is a comparison, a *tertium comparationis*, an analogy. Nevertheless Freud conceded that the notion of the symbol is not yet precisely defined and it is often confused with substitution, representation, and even allusion.

We feel, however, that there remains no doubt as to the general nature of its substance. In other words, it is a trace of manifested content which has a correspondence to the latent content of dreams. Because censure prohibits the projection of this latent element in its integral form, the libido authorizes its being displaced. In disguised form this latent element penetrates the ballroom of dreams where a multitude of other elements dance an apparently disordered orgy, stimulating at times feelings such as anxiety, fear, and fright.

We cannot avoid being astonished at those who call themselves psychoanalytical folklorists and who do not know the following studies of Freud: *The Interpretation of Dreams* and *A General Introduction to Psychoanalysis*. We feel that reading these studies is essential. Above all, through them will be learned how the elaboration of dreams takes place (a process for the conversion of the latent content into the manifested one) and how to analyze dreams (the contrary task which accomplishes a reverse transformation). They will also learn the meaning of many symbols including those which transcend the boundaries of language and occur in man the world over.

Let us then look at an abbreviated view of this Freudian chapter on the "language of dreams," attempting to partially recapitulate it in outline form:

I. Symbols of the human body:
  (1) Houses with smooth walls=men
  (2) Houses with projections and balconies=women
II. Symbols of parents:
  (3) The emperor and the empress, the king and the queen, and items like that
III. Symbols of sons and daughters, brothers or sisters:
  (4) Small animals and parasites
IV. Symbols of birth:
  (5) Water
V. Symbols of death:
  (6) The departure or a railroad trip
  (7) Various dark and sinister signs
VI. Symbols of nudity:
  (8) Suits and uniforms
VII. Symbols of the male genital organs:
  (9) The number 3
  (10) Machines which are difficult to describe
  (11) Fire
  (12) Various tools, the plough
VIII. Symbols of the penis in particular:
  (13) Canes, umbrellas, stalks, trees
  (14) Painted arms of all kinds, knives, daggers, lances, and sabers
  (15) Firearms, rifles, pistols, revolvers
  (16) Faucets, jars, jets of water
  (17) Hanging lamps, mechanical pencils
  (18) Pencils, toothpick cases, nail files, hammers
  (19) Globes, airplanes, and dirigibles
  (20) Oneiric flights
  (21) Reptiles and fishes, the snake
  (22) The hat, the coat
  (23) The foot, the hand
IX. Symbols of the feminine genital organs:
  (24) Mines, ditches, caverns, vases and bottles, boxes of all shapes, coffers, chests, pockets
  (25) The boat
  (26) The mouth, the ear, the eye
  (27) Snails, bivalvular shellfish
  (28) Scenery with boulders, woods, and water

(29) Jewelry box
(30) Woods, the table
(31) Flowers, the garden
(32) The boot, the slipper
(33) The horseshoe

X.   Symbol of the maternal breast in particular:
(34) Closets, stoves
(35) Rooms

XI. Symbols of access to the sexual orifice:
(36) The door, the portal

XII. Symbols of hair around the genital organs of both sexes:
(37) Woods, forests

XIII. Symbols of sexual pleasure:
(38) Sweets

XIV. Symbols of sexual pleasure obtained without recourse to a second individual:
(39) Games of all kinds
(40) The act of playing the piano
(41) Slipping, rapid descent, the breaking of a branch

XV. Symbols of castration considered as punishment for hidden practices:
(42) A fall or the extraction of a molar

XVI. Symbols of sexual intercourse:
(43) Rhythmic activities, dancing, horseback riding, ascending
(44) Specific violent accidents such as being struck by a vehicle
(45) Certain manual activities
(46) Being threatened by a weapon
(47) The stairway or ramp and the act of climbing them (29:26)

Pôrto-Carrero also systematizes a framework of very interesting oneiric symbols in his *A psicologia profunda ou psicandlise,* although he does not fully explain his basis of classification (55). Jung, in his celebrated *Transformations and Symbols of the Libido,* treats the most frequent symbols of the "collective unconscious" comparatively (44).

The reader must not think that the analysis of a dream is carried out in a simplistic manner just by consulting this list of best known symbols. This would relegate the problem to its former condition

—the prediction of dreams, fortunetelling, and cartomancy. It would mean relegating the interpretation of symbols to the most prelogical solutions of folklore itself.

Folklore cannot be left out of the prediction of dreams. In Paraguay "To dream about broken teeth—is a misfortune; about scanty hair—bodes ill; about a knife—augurs ill; that he falls—is a bad augury; with a black woman—is bad fortune; that he is climbing—is a good augury; about abundant hair—bodes well; about clear water—is happy success; about a brunette—is good fortune; that a person has died—that you will live many years; about white hair—a letter" (17).

From Uruguay, for example, we know that "To dream about a little baby is disloyalty—twenty-eight is played in the quiniela. To dream about an egg—the double zero is played in the quiniela. When you dream about a dead person talking, play forty-eight. To dream about dirty water means blood. Teeth falling out means a relative's death. Money means fleas and fleas mean money" (18).

In other areas examples on this topic are even in verse, like the following sample of folklore from Sergipe, Brazil:

> To dream about an old woman or a dead man,
> a duck, a chicken or a turkey,
> or any feathered bird,
> or thing bearing a cross,
> is without a doubt
> a sign of winning with an ostrich.
>
> If you dream about a swindler,
> about water and people in mourning,
> about a tall and barren woman,
> wrinkled and hardheaded,
> and if you bet on the eagle,
> you'll win lots of money.
>
> When in your dream there appears
> an enormous grass field,
> a doctor with many books
> carrying a briefcase
> the animal that wins is a donkey,
> There is nothing more certain than that* (66:17).

The task of analyzing dreams is very complex and cannot be

*These verses pertain to "jôgo do bicho," a game of chance played with animal symbols.

accomplished without a methodology of free association of ideas. On more than one occasion Freud cautions that the application and translation of these symbols is less simple than what may be supposed (26). Consequently, in psychoanalytical folklore great care is needed to avoid interpretations which are not in harmony with the cultural milieu of the material being analyzed.

STRUCTURE OF THE PSYCHIC SYSTEM

In addition to the idea of infant sexuality, Freud developed such original and revolutionary concepts as those surrounding the psychic system. Here his contribution was the development of the idea of the unconscious. To discuss this concept now is not surprising. The history of psychoanalysis, however, points out how many obstacles Freud had to overcome to uphold infant sexuality, the unconscious, and other principles against academic psychologists. It was like Columbus in the presence of the pythagorean scholars of the University of Salamanca defending his theory of going to the Orient by going west.

Freud expounds his thesis on the mental structure in several works. The following are essential to the development of this topic: *Metapsychology* (1913–1917), *Beyond the Pleasure Principle* (1920), and *The Ego and the Id* (1923). At the outset their author states that the psychic system is made up of three principal parts: the conscious, the unconscious, and the preconscious. The conscious is the place where current ideas reside. From time to time these ideas take flight: they are transitory. Most of the time it is sufficient to remember them for them to reappear. In such cases we do not need new sensory stimuli. This is proof positive that they do not depart from or leave the person. Where then do they remain during their absence?

It must have been this type of speculation which led Freud to establish his first outline of the psychic system. According to him our absent ideas rest in a mental compartment behind the conscious: the unconscious or nonconscious. The proof of the existence of the unconscious is provided by memory, and even more by hypnosis and dreams. Continuing his investigations Freud studied the contents of the unconscious and discovered that some items could become conscious voluntarily while others could not. He then resolved that those items which could easily enter the conscious, that is, by one's own free will, were located in a part of the unconscious known as the preconscious. Those incapable of easy recollection are deeply buried in the unconscious and can only be drawn out by very special methods which make up the science of psychoanalysis. It is for this reason that this science has merited the label of "psychology of the depths" (*Tiefenpsychologie*).

Freud later completed his first outline of the psychic system by developing the ideas of the ego, the superego, and the id. He called this his second outline of the psychic system. The ego contains both the contents of the conscious and the preconscious. It is the social phase of the psyche. The id contains repressed ideas in the unconscious. The superego is unconscious censorship and is characterized by norms of moral perfection. It is the ideal ego or the ideal of the ego.

We could put it this way: the ego equates with what the individual feigns to be, the id corresponds to what he really is, and the superego to what he hopes to be. Consequently the superego can punish the ego when the latter gives in to the principle of pleasure to the detriment of the principle of reality. It is the superego that develops feelings of guilt which can lead the ego to suicide. In the legend of Oedipus the self-punishment of the oedipal ego resulted in his tearing out his own eyes; Jocasta hung herself.

To explain the correlation of the two Freudian outlines of the psychic system, Dalbiez prepared a frame of correspondences which I am copying here because of its usefulness. Dalbiez explains that the ego includes conscious and preconscious elements, that is, numbers 1 and 2 in his outline. The superego is the unconscious repressor, number 3. The id corresponds to the unconscious repressed, or number 4.

```
Conscious Psychic Processes..............................1 ⎫
                                                          ⎬ The Ego
                      ⎡ Preconscious.....................2 ⎭
                      ⎢ (capable of being
                      ⎢ voluntarily recalled)
Unconscious ⎨ Unconscious
Psychic       ⎢ (incapable of being  ⎡ Repressor   3   The Superego
Processes:    ⎢ voluntarily          ⎣ Repressed   4   The id
                      ⎣ recalled)
```

MECHANISMS OF THE PSYCHIC SYSTEM

The mental structure referred to is clearer if observed in full operation. Freud attached the mechanism of the psychic system to its step by step operation. He speculated, for example, on why certain aspects of the unconscious could be voluntarily brought to consciousness and others not. This inevitably led him to develop the idea of censorship. Censorship is like a judge sitting between the unconscious and the conscious. It functions like a customs house, either permitting or denying access to the normal passage or to the bootlegging of ideas from the unconscious to the preconscious, and from the latter to consciousness under pressure from the libido.

The interdict imposed by censorship is a mechanism properly labeled repression. Consequently the unconscious is the storage place of repressed ideas as well as those which are merely latent. When psychoanalytical techniques attempt to bring repressed ideas to the surface, the repression which forced them into the unconscious transforms itself into resistance. Resistance is another psychic mechanism and its purpose is to prevent the unconscious from becoming conscious whenever we feel obliged to do so. Psychoanalytical techniques consist in subordinating resistance, extracting repressed material from the depths of the unconscious, and bringing it to the surface of consciousness.

An understanding of censorship, repression, and resistance leads us to other mechanisms of the psychic system, above all that of sublimation. For clarity's sake this concept is dealt with in conjunction with the notion of the pleasure principle and the principle of reality. The pleasure principle rules the libido while the principle of reality rules censorship. Social life is a permanent superposition of the principle of reality over the pleasure principle. This causes a constant set of egocentric restrictions, limitations, and grief. The principle of reality is fundamentally disagreeable. The child with oedipal inclinations has to forego his claims on his mother because of this principle.

Finally, the existence of the principle of reality is understood as social control (repression). With this control the capacity for censorship is developed. This will later become the superego. The superego therefore stems from the perception of the principle of reality and also from identification. That is to say, the individual not only complies with the principle of reality but he does so by emulating a model with whom he identifies. This model may be his father or another person who appears to him to be a model of perfection (social perfection). The boy's ambivalent feelings for his father originate here. He hates him as a sexual rival, but he loves him as a result of wishing to be like him.

The effects of censorship on the libido can then be either extensive or without effect. If they are extensive the libido becomes detoured or repressed. The repressed libido goes to the depths of the unconscious. A detoured libido is what Freud labeled as the mechanism of sublimation.

Sublimation is controlled by another principle which I take the risk of calling the principle of compensation. The individual does not possess his mother (Oedipus complex) but in compensation he possesses another woman. He has not been able to knife people in the streets (sadism) but in compensation he becomes a surgeon. He has not been able to play at being a mother (maternal instinct) but in compensation he becomes a philanthropist. He has not been able to continue to cherish his anus (anal complex) but in compensation he is a miser. According to Roger Bastide such correlations are now prevalent in psychoanalytical studies by Jones, Bovet, Baudoin, and others (26:33). Artists, religious figures, and orators, to name but a few, are explained in this way. I believe that the concept of sublimation is indispensible in folkloric casuistry. Many tales, legends, and beliefs are nothing more than examples of detoured libido.

The following Freudian interpretations provide even greater clarity on the structure and mechanisms of the psychic system: "Now let us call 'conscious' the conception which is present to our consciousness and of which we are aware, and let this be the only meaning of the term 'conscious.' As for latent conceptions, if we have any reason to suppose that they exist in the mind—as we had in the case of memory—let them be denoted by the term 'unconscious.' Thus an unconscious conception is one of which we are not aware, but the existence of which we are nevertheless ready to admit on account of other proofs or signs" (32:22–23).

"We learn therefore by the analysis of neurotic phenomena that a latent or unconscious idea is not necessarily a weak one, and that the presence of such an idea in the mind admits of indirect proofs of the most cogent kind, which are equivalent to the direct proof furnished by consciousness. We feel justified in making our classification agree with this addition to our knowledge by introducing a fundamental distinction between different kinds of latent or unconscious ideas. We are accustomed to think that every latent idea was so because it was weak and that it grew conscious as soon as it became strong. We have now gained the conviction that there are some latent ideas which do not penetrate into consciousness, however strong they may have become. Therefore we may call the latent ideas of the first type *foreconscious*, while we reserve the term *unconscious* (proper) for the latter type which we came to study in the neuroses. The term *unconscious*, which was used in the purely descriptive sense before, now comes to imply something more. It designates not only latent ideas in general, but especially ideas with a certain dynamic character, ideas keeping apart from consciousness in spite of their intensity and activity" (32:262).

"It is by no means impossible for the product of unconscious activity to pierce into consciousness, but a certain amount of exertion is needed for this task. When we try to do it in ourselves, we become aware of a distinct feeling of *repulsion* which must be overcome, and when we produce it in a patient we get the more unquestionable signs of what we call his *resistance* to it. So we learn that the unconscious idea is excluded from consciousness by living forces which oppose themselves to its reception, while they do not object to other ideas, the foreconscious ones" (32a:263–264).

"The distinction between foreconscious and unconscious activity is not a primary one, but comes to be established after repulsion has sprung up. Only then the difference between foreconscious ideas, which can appear in consciousness and reappear at any moment, and unconscious ideas which cannot do so gains a theoretical as well as a practical value" (32a:264).

"It has consequently become a condition of repression that the motive force of unpleasure shall have acquired more strength than the pleasure obtained from satisfaction. Psychoanalytic observation of the transference neuroses, morever, leads us to conclude that repression is not a defensive mechanism which is present from the very beginning, and that it cannot arise until a sharp cleavage has occurred between conscious and unconscious mental activity—that the essence of repression lies *simply in turning something away and keeping it at a distance, from the complete consciousness"* (32:147).

"Everything that is repressed must remain unconscious; but let us state at the very outset that the repressed does not cover everything that is unconscious. The unconscious has the wider compass: the repressed is a part of the unconscious.

"How are we to arrive at a knowledge of the unconscious? It is of course only as something conscious that we know it, after it has undergone transformation or translation into something conscious. Psycho-analytic work shows us every day that translation of this kind is possible. In order that this should come about, the person under analysis must overcome certain resistances—the very same resistances as those which, earlier, made the material concerned into something repressed by rejecting it from the conscious" (32:166).

"The unconscious comprises, on the one hand, acts which are merely latent, temporarily unconscious, but which differ in no other respect from conscious ones and, on the other hand, processes such repressed ones, which if they were to become conscious would be bound to stand out in the crudest contrast to the rest of the conscious processes" (32:172).

"Proceeding now to an account of the positive findings of psychoanalysis, we now may say that in general a psychical act goes through two phases as regards its state, between which is interposed a kind of testing (censorship). In the first phase the psychical act is unconscious and belongs to the system *Ucs:* if, on testing, it is rejected by the censorship, it is not allowed to pass into the second phase; it is then said to be 'repressed' and must remain unconscious. If, however, it passes this testing, it enters the second phase and thenceforth belongs to the second system, which we will call the system *Cs.* But the fact that it belongs to that system does not yet unequivocally determine its relation to consciousness. It is not yet conscious, but it is certainly *capable of becoming conscious* . . . that is, it can now, given certain conditions, become an object of consciousness without any special resistance. In consideration of this capacity for becoming conscious we also call the system *Cs* the 'preconscious.' If it should turn out that a certain censorship also plays a part in determining whether the preconscious becomes conscious, we shall discriminate more sharply between the systems *Pcs* and *Cs* . . . For the present let it suffice us to bear in mind that the system *Pcs* shares the characteristics of the system *Cs* and that the rigorous censorship exercises its office at the point of transition from the *Ucs* to the *Pcs* (or *Cs*).

"By accepting the existence of these two (or three) psychical systems, psycho-analysis has departed a step further from the descriptive 'psychology of consciousness' and has raised new problems and acquired a new content. Up till now, it has differed from that psychology mainly by reason of its *dynamic* view of mental processes; now in addition it seems to take account of psychical topography as well, and to indicate in respect of any given mental act within what system or between what systems it takes place. On account of this attempt, too, it has been given the name of 'depth-psychology' (32:172–173).

"To most people who have been educated in philosophy the idea of anything psychical which is not also conscious is so inconceivable that it seems to them absurd and refutable simply by logic. I believe this is only because they have never studied the relevant phenomena of hypnosis and dreams, which—quite apart from pathological manifestations—necessitate this view. Their psychology of consciousness is incapable of solving the problems of dreams and hypnosis.

" 'Being conscious' is in the first place a purely descriptive term, resting on perception of the most immediate and certain character. Experience goes on to show that a psychical element (for instance, an idea) is not as a rule conscious for a protracted length of time. On the contrary, a state of consciousness is characteristically very transitory" (26:3–4).

"Thus we obtain our concept of the unconscious from the theory of repression. The repressed is the prototype of the unconscious for us. We see, however, that we have two kinds of unconscious—the one which is latent but capable of becoming conscious, and the one which is repressed and which is not, in itself and without more ado, capable of becoming conscious. This piece of insight into psychical dynamics cannot fail to affect terminology and description. The latent, which is unconscious only descriptively, not in the dynamic sense, we call *preconscious;* we restrict the term *unconscious* to the dynamically unconscious repressed; so that now we have three terms, conscious (*Cs*), preconscious (*Pcs*), and unconscious (*Ucs*), whose sense is no longer purely descriptive" (26:5).

"The question which we put off answering runs as follows: How is it that the superego manifests itself essentially as a sense of guilt (or rather, as criticism—for the sense of guilt is the perception in the ego answering to this criticism) and moreover develops such extraordinary harshness and severity towards the ego? If we turn to melancholia first, we find that the excessively strong superego which has obtained a hold upon consciousness rages against the ego with merciless violence, as if it had taken possesion of the whole of the sadism available in the person concerned. Following our view of sadism, we should say that the destructive component had entrenched itself in the superego and turned against the ego. What is now holding sway in the superego is, as it were, a pure culture of the death instinct, and in fact it often enough succeeds in driving the ego into death, if the latter does not fend off its tyrant in time by the change around into mania. The reproaches of conscience in certain forms of obsessional neurosis are as distressing and tormenting, but here the situation is less perspicuous" (26:43).

"The superego arises, as we know, from an identification with the father taken as a model (26:44)." "We see this same ego as a poor creature owing service to three masters and consequently menaced by three dangers: from the external world, from the libido of the id, and from the severity of the superego. Three kinds of anxiety correspond to these three dangers, since anxiety is the expression of a retreat from danger" (26:46).

4

The Collective Unconscious

Let us now add the contributions of Jung, the heterodox psychoanalyst, to the Freudian metapsychology. We are indebted to the head of the Swiss school for very profound and original psychological concepts. His ideas on the "collective unconscious" are of primary importance to psychoanalytical folklorists. He expressed these in more than one work but principally in *Transformations and Symbols of the Libido* (1912), *Psychological Types* (1921), *The Relations Between the Ego and the Unconscious* (1928), and *Psychology and Religion* (1940).

For those who already know Jung's position with respect to his mentor, a frankly emancipated one, it is important to note that in dealing with the concept of the collective unconscious Jung complements Freud rather than opposing him. For Jung the concept of the unconscious is an exclusively psychological concept, and not a philosophical concept in the sense of being something metaphysical. The unconscious is a psychologically bound concept which includes all content which is not concerned with the ego. He adopts an independent position by refusing to accept the Freudian unconscious as such. According to Jung the Freudian unconscious is solely the "personal unconscious" (42).

In other words, Jung established the existence of a total unconscious which is divided into two parts: the personal unconscious, where repressed ideas are stored, and the collective unconscious which does not store repressed ideas but rather archetypes or archaic contents. It is worth noting that these ideas exist hereditarily. He labeled them collective because he felt they were universal images—symbols which all humanity possesses.

ARCHETYPES AND FUNDAMENTAL IDEAS

To pursue the idea further is to realize that the Jungian archetypes are essentially a new version of Bastian's fundamental ideas (Elementargedanken). This suggestion is not a backward step away from the solution of the problem since both archetypes and fundamental ideas were placed in the unconscious by Jung. This permits the statement that human minds are identical in the unconscious. It would have been a backward step indeed if these elements were located in the conscious, since it would be absurd to affirm that human minds are identical in the conscious.

In my opinion Jung complemented Bastian, Tylor, Lévy-Bruhl, and the anthropologists of his time who in general had not internalized the concept of the unconscious. In fact, Bastian's fundamental ideas referred to the conscious. They were ideas common to mankind the world over which he possesses without ever recalling having learned them from anyone. Tylor concluded from this that they had developed from a supposed identity of the human mind (*Quod ubique, quod semper, quod ab omnibus*), and from that assumption the famous theory of convergence was created. Lévy-Bruhl rebelled against such identity and attempted to demonstrate the existence of prelogical and logical mentalities, fundamental principles for his historical-cultural theory.

Of course, Jung complemented their work since from any point of view he used these scholars as points of departure. He adapted the notion of fundamental ideas to the unconscious while he relegated only the logical and prelogical mentalities to the conscious. Human minds would then be identical in the unconscious (collective unconscious) and nonidentical in the conscious. Jung served as a bridge between these old anthropological schools, Tylor's English one and the French one of Lévy-Bruhl. Even his "nondirected thought" is nothing more than the "prelogical mentality" of Lévy-Bruhl.

The outline of his plan is as follows:

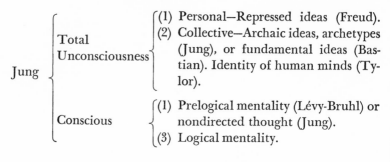

NONDIRECTED THOUGHT
AND PRELOGICAL MENTALITY

To demonstrate the similarity of Jung's nondirected thought and Lévy-Bruhl's prelogical mentality, let us examine the specifics of Jung's explanation. The reader should consult my *Concept of Folklore* for the specifics of Lévy-Bruhl's explanation. (15) This similarity begins with the very title of the chapter in which Jung studies the topic: "The Two Methods of Thought." It brings Lévy-Bruhl and his two patterns of mentality vividly to mind. The two methods of thought are directed thought and nondirected thought:

". . . directed or logical thinking is reality thinking, a thinking that is adapted to reality, by means of which we imitate the successiveness of objectively real things, so that the images inside our mind follow one another in the same strictly causal sequence as the events taking place outside it. We also call this "thinking with directed attention." It has in addition the peculiarity of causing fatigue, and is for that reason brought into play for short periods only. The whole laborious achievement of our lives is adaptation to reality, part of which consists in directed thinking. In biological terms it is simply a process of psychic assimilation that leaves behind a corresponding state of exhaustion, like any other vital achievement.

"The material with which we think is *language and verbal concepts*—something which from time immemorial has been directed outwards and used as a bridge, and which has but a single purpose, namely that of communication. So long as we think directly, we think *for* others and speak *to* others" (44:11–12).

The other thought, on the other hand, the so-called nondirected or dreams or even fantasy, is associative, subjective, fantastic par excellence. "The latter form, if not constantly corrected by adapted thinking, is bound to produce an overwhelmingly subjective and distorted picture of the world. This state of mind has been described in the first place as infantile and autoerotic, or, with Bleuler, as "autistic," which clearly expresses the view that the subjective picture, judged from the standpoint of adaptation, is inferior to that of directed thinking. The ideal instance of autism is found in schizophrenia, whereas infantile autoeroticism is more characteristic of neurosis. Such a view brings a perfectly normal process like non-directed fantasy-thinking dangerously close to the pathological" (44:28).

NIETZSCHE: DREAMS AND MYTHS

Nietzsche's ideas in his famous *Human, Too Human* are thus understandable: "While sleeping and dreaming we redo all the tasks of primitive humanity." Primitive humanity or "young humanity," as it is called by Freud, or even the "infantile psychic behavior of the people," K. Abraham's term, are roughly equivalent.

Nietzsche continues: "In sleep and in dreams we pass through the whole thought of earlier humanity. . . . What I mean is this: as man now reasons in dreams, so humanity also reasoned for many thousands of years when awake; the first cause which occurred to the mind as an explanation of anything that required explanation was sufficient and passed for truth. . . . This atavistic element in man's nature still manifests itself in our dreams, for it is the foundation upon which the higher reason has developed and still develops in every individual. Dreams carry us back to remote conditions of human culture and give us a ready means of understanding them better. Dream thinking comes so easily to us now because this form of fantastic and facile explanation in terms of the first random idea has been drilled into us for immense periods of time. To that extent dreaming is a recreation for the brain, which by day has to satisfy the stern demands of thought imposed by a higher culture. . . .

"From this we can see how *lately* the more acute logical thinking, the strict discrimination of cause and effect, has been developed, since our rational and intellectual faculties still involuntarily hark back to those primitive forms of reasoning, and we pass about half our lives in this condition" (44:23–24).

In other words the myth is the secular and collective dream of the psychic behavior of the people (Jung), while the dream is the myth of the individual (K. Abraham). The myth was formerly the principal means of thinking. Nondirected thought prevailed then and it was loaded with folkloric archetypes. Little by little psychic behavior learned to direct itself and in so doing to stop being infantile. Directed thought does not dream, "imagine", or manipulate myths. A technical people, while being technical, rejects myths and does not support collective and secular dreams. Technology is an accomplishment of directed thought. Myths inhabit the psyche, as much on the part of the individual as of humanity, only because mental fatigue overcomes the continual efforts of directing thought. An individual tires and so does an entire people. In such a condition the contents of the unconscious mind move over and occupy the place of the conscious one. Ancestral images people the present, become dominant. Because of this they are called archetypes or dominant figures.

ARCHETYPES AND NEUROTIC
HALLUCINATIONS

Jung advanced his investigations even further. He considered again the old statement that folklore is likely to appear in dreams and neuroses (statements of former colleagues) and he tried to develop an explanation for this through the concept of archetypes. Neurotic hallucinations in this case may be reflections of the collective unconscious of the sick person himself. He supposes he sees and speaks to monsters, wild beasts, witches, charmed people, and ghosts. Such was the clinical record of Jung's patient Miss Frank Miller, a record which was traced throughout his study *Transformations and Symbols of the Libido* (1912). This work could have well received the subtitle: "The Clinical Record of Miss Frank Miller." The symbols of this patient's libido are carefully described and interpreted. Due to the concept of archetypes, much of Miss Miller's record could be man's folkloric heredity.

JUNG: ONTOGENESIS RECAPITULATES PHYLOGENESIS

Jung advanced one step further by stating that ontogenesis recapitulates phylogenesis in the psychic realm also. This means that the genesis of the individual is the reproduction of the genesis of the species. If we wish to investigate the species we must examine the individual. The processes of embryonic transformations the individual goes through have been the processes humanity has gone through since its origin. In other words, the child's thought is paleontological man's thought. And since this paleontological man in our times finds his likeness in the primitive or the savage, the conclusion is then drawn that children and primitives think alike. This thinking is nondirected, prelogical, mythological, autistic.

THE FOLKLORIC UNCONSCIOUS

The last step was taken by Ramos. In considering the characteristics of archetypes—gods, demons, magicians, witch doctors, ghosts, loupgarous of all epochs, all the myths, all the folklores—he did not hesitate to propose a synonym for the Jungian unconscious, designating it the folkloric unconscious (59:329, 330). He continued to use this term which he had proposed at the beginning of his studies, that is, in his first work, *Primitivo e loucura* (1926) (62:88).

Research in archetypes was for Ramos one of the principal missions of folkloric science. These are, he states, "structural contexts which lead us to an understanding of our collective psyche." He avers that a social psychology which does not investigate the relationship between the evident forms of culture and their unconscious contexts is descriptive social psychology, superficial, *ad usum delphini*. It must go further. It must proceed from the analysis of prelogical categories of a cycle of civilization by investigating the folkloric unconscious (57:275–276).

It seems to Ramos for this reason that we are not yet ready to understand the collective psyche of the Brazilian. We are not because psychoanalytical folklore studies are still few and inadequate. We still need to know the historical truth about Brazil— not the data contained in "biographies or political episodes, automatic and stereotyped history without relation to the ethnic masses, but rather another one, more exact, more scientific, of the ordeals and transformations of the folkloric unconscious" (60:409–410).

Ramos suggests that the history of the Brazilian folkloric unconscious could never be written by the "doctors and scholars with their trips to Europe and their erudite conferences and who live among us by the dozens." Never, "because they are individualists and live separated from the masses. More than ever, we must penetrate the masses and dissolve the cement, unbraid the forces of participation, and understand the libidinal substratum of mana" (60:408).

JUNGIAN TEXTS

The following Jungian texts are the most expressive and deal in particular with the collective unconscious: "Besides the obvious personal sources, creative fantasy also draws upon the forgotten and long buried primitive mind with its host of images, which are to be found in the mythologies of all ages and all peoples. The sum of these images constitutes the collective unconscious, a heritage which is potentially present in every individual" (44:29).

"We have therefore, two kinds of thinking: directed thinking, and dreaming or fantasy-thinking. The former operates with speech elements for the purpose of communication, and is difficult and exhausting; the latter is effortless, working as it were spontaneously, with the contents ready to hand, and guided by unconscious motives. The one produces innovations and adaptations, copies reality, and tries to act upon it; the other turns away from reality, sets free subjective tendencies, and as regards adaptation, is unproductive.

"As I have indicated above, history shows that directed thinking was not always as developed as it is today. The clearest expression of modern directed thinking is science and the techniques fostered by it. Both owe their existence simply and solely to energetic training in directed thinking" (44:18–19).

"Whereas directed thinking is an altogether conscious phenomenon, the same cannot be said of fantasy-thinking. Much of it belongs to the conscious sphere, but at least as much goes on in the half-shadow, or entirely in the unconscious, and can therefore be inferred only indirectly" (44:29).

"All this shows how much the products of the unconscious have in common with mythology. We should therefore have to conclude that any introversion occurring in later life regresses back to infantile reminiscences which, though derived from the individual's past, generally have a slight archaic tinge. With stronger introversion and regression the archaic features become more pronounced" (44:30).

"This rule can be applied to the mythological tradition in general: it does not perpetuate accounts of ordinary events in the past, but only of those which express the universal and ever-renewed thoughts of mankind. Thus the lives and deeds of the culture-heroes and founders of religions are the purest condensations of typical mythological motifs, behind which the individual figures entirely disappear" (44:31).

Jung says that experience also teaches us that there are unconscious psychic connections, mythological images, for example, which never have been part of the conscious, and these must trace their origin to unconscious activity. Furthermore, the experience about the nature of unconscious contexts permits us to use a general kind of classification. We can distinguish a personal unconscious which includes all the attainments of personal life, that is, everything which was forgotten, repressed, perceived, thought, and felt at the threshold of conscience. In addition to such personal unconscious contexts there are others which do not stem from personal attainments but rather from the inherited cerebral structure. These are the mythological connections, the motives and images, which can reappear at any time or any place without historical tradition or previous migration. These contexts are considered the collective unconscious (44).

"In view of these facts we must assume that the unconscious contains not only personal, but also impersonal, collective components in the form of inherited categories or archetypes. I have therefore advanced the hypothesis that at its deeper levels the unconscious possesses collective contents in a relatively active state. That is why I speak of the collective unconscious" (42:135).

"The personal grows out of the collective psyche and is intimately bound to it. So it is difficult to say exactly what contents are to be called personal and what collective. There is no doubt, for instance, that archaic symbolisms such as we frequently find in fantasies and dreams are collective factors. All basic instincts and basic forms of thought and feeling are collective. Everything that all men agree in regarding as universal is collective, likewise everything that is universally understood, universally found, universally said and done" (43:152).

"The theory of preconscious primordial ideas is by no means my own invention, as the term 'archetype,' which stems from the first centuries of our era, proves. With special reference to psychology we find this theory in the works of Adolf Bastian and then again in Nietzsche. In French literature Hubert and Mauss, and also Lévy-Bruhl, mention similar ideas. I only gave an empirical foundation to the theory of what were formerly called primordial or elementary ideas, 'categories' or *habitudes directrices de la conscience,* 'collective representations,' etc., by setting out to investigate certain details" (41:50–51).

Part Three: Case Studies

5

Oral Libido

Following the pattern I have used before for the explanation of these theories I now refer the reader to the corresponding examples. Perhaps everything will appear too organized, too perfectly classified; hence this explanation.

An appearance of absolute organization is a personal necessity, without which my work would lack order. I had recourse to a system which, for lack of another name, I call the criterion of predominance. In order to classify an item I took into consideration its most outstanding psychoanalytic characteristic. There are at times three or four psychoanalytical aspects by which the item could be identified. The reader will understand, therefore, that if I had not taken into consideration more than a single aspect—the predominant one—we would have a needless, bothersome, and even confusing repetition of examples.

Using this criterion then, I will refer to fragment X in, for example, the frame of oral libido, and only in it, although I could probably also do so in my citations on the Oedipus complex.

Lexical stereotypes, neologisms, verbal formulas, and mimicry—which appear not only in rounds, songs, and children's games, but also in the language of lunatics and primitive men—are manifestations of folkloric concern about the oral libido. This libido characterizes the human being in a phase when he is the depository of tendencies and impulses which seek their fulfillment in a disorderly way, (63:194) Bastide places ritual cannibalism of indigenous Australians and their communion meals in the classification of oral libido (4:80, 108–110).

LEXICAL STEREOTYPES

Lexical stereotypes are phenomena of the language characterized by suggestibility, imitation, and mental automatism. (63:136) Rodolfo Senet studied these thoroughly in his basic work *Las estoglosias.* (65) Ramos studied them jointly in children, lunatics, and savages. In folklore we are obviously only interested in lexical stereotypes of normal children and adults particularly when they contain tradition, anonymity, and so on.

Embolalia is clearly one of these stereotypes. It consists in adding syllables to a word as if they were prefixes or suffixes or even to insert or join words and phrases to each other without any meaning. Folklorically speaking the following types of acts are embolalias:

A. Language using pp's, ff's, or rr's.
B. Language using repetitive final syllables.
C. Language with a sequenced syllable omission.
D. Language of metathesis.
E. The embolalia of refrains.

In Uruguay embolalia is called *jerigonza* or jargon. In Brazil it is called *linguagem embolada.* There are even songs known as *embolada* because they are very difficult to sing. Examples of type A:

(1) Euferreu gosfarrós toforró deferrê doforrô ceferrê.

This means *Eu gosto de doce* (I like sweets) (63:173).

(2) Buepe nopos dipi apas.
     Buefe nofos difi afas.

This becomes *Buenos días* (good-day, hello). The same thing can be accomplished by substituting an entire word for the *p* or the *f.* For example, using the word *campana,* the above expression would appear this way:

(3) Buecampana noscampanas dicampanas ascampanas.

Although my informant assures me that common jargon is most frequently accomplished with the *p* and the *f* in Uruguay, he mentioned that a limitless number of codes can nevertheless be developed.

(4) Un genereito lindeito barateito.

This means "Un género lindo, barato" (A pretty cheap cloth).

There is a Brazilian style for the use of final syllables. It consists in taking as a convention the final syllable of a word used in the sentence and using it as the embolalia. If the children, for example, see one who is not a part of their group they sing:

> (5) Meninoíno
> Catibiribino
> Serramatipino
> Foroforofino

When they see a youngster with a *touca* (cap) they chant:

> (6) Toucaouca
> Catibiribouca
> Serramatipouca
> Foroforofouca.

Were it a *cavalo* (horse), they would say:

> (7) Cavaloalo
> Catibiribalo
> Serramatipalo
> Foroforofalo.

Up until now we have only illustrated embolalia by the addition of syllables and letters. The contrary phenomena also occurs in folklore.

(8) Um ca, sê bô, dô nê.

This is an item of infantine folklore from Sergipe, Brazil, which means *Um carro, seis bois, dois negros* (A cart, six oxen, two Negroes).

(9) Um tá
tu tu ti nu té
um tá na tá na tom
e ôto até o té

This is also from the folklore of Sergipe and states: Um pau/com um cupim no pé/ um gravatá na ponta/ e ôco até o pé (A stick, with a termite at its bottom, moss on its tip, and hollow to the end). Even reverse speech exists.

> (10) Mosvá arsepás jehô?

This is an example from the folklore of Minas Gerais which asks *Vamos passear hoje?* (Are we going for a walk today?).

From the embolalia of song refrains I recall this Brazilian children's round:

> (11) Bom dia, meu senhorio,   (A very good day, sir.
>   Manda o tiro-tiro-lá. (63:173):   From the tiro-tiro-la.

Variations on this theme are numerous in the Rio de la Plata region.

> (12) Buenos días, su señoría,   (Good day, sir.
>   Aquí me manda el rey de Hungría. The King of Hungary
>   sent me here.
>
>   Buenos días, su señoría   Good day, sir,
>   Mantantiru lirolá. (36:54)   From the tiru lirolá.)

Hundreds of songs, rounds, and games from the world's folklore which so delight the inner life of the child can be relegated to this species. Children find in them an escape for the energy of their oral libido. Without consulting other bibliographical sources we will quote from Garibaldi's anthology since it is so rich in examples from America and Spain which are true to the oral tradition (36).

> (13) En Francia nace un niño
>   chiribín, chiribín, chin, chin.
>   (In France a child is born.)
>   chiribin, chiribin, chin, chin.

> (14) Se me ha perdido una hija,
>   cataplín, cataplín, cataplero.
>   Se me ha perdido una hija
>   en el fondo del jardín.
>   (One of my daughters was lost,)
>   Cataplín, cataplín cataplero,
>   (One of my daughters was lost
>   In the back of the garden.)

(15) Yo tengo una buena torre,
latarimbarimbarón.
Yo tengo una buena torre,
latarimbarimbarón.
(I have a fine tower,)
latarimbarimbarón.
(I have a fine tower,)
latarimbarimbarón.

(16) ¿Adónde va la niña coja?
chirunflín, chirunflán.
¿Adónde va la niña coja?
la murín con trán.
(Where is the crippled girl going?)
chirunflín, chirunflán.
(Where is the crippled girl going?) ,
la murín con trán.

(17) Estaba la pastora,
larán, larán, larito.
estaba la pastora,
cuidando un rebañito.
(There was once a shepherdess.)
larán, larán, larito.
(There was once a shepherdess,
Caring for a little herd.)

I have only quoted a pair of verses or a quartet from each piece.
Let us use the ballad *Había una vieja* (There was once an old
lady) as a paradigm to get an idea of how these are developed.

(18) Habia una vieja   (There was once an old lady,
virueja, virueja,   orold, orold,
de pico picotueja   with a mouth, mouthold,
de pomporirá.   with a pomporira.)

Tenía tres hijos,   (She had three children,
virijo, virijo,   chirildren, chirildren,
de pico, picotijo,   with a mouth, mouthildren,
de pomporirá.   with a pomporira.)

Uno iba a la escuela   (One went to school
viruela, viruela,   schurool, schurool,,
de pico picotuela   with a mouth, mouthool,
de pomporirá.   with a pomporira.)

Otro iba al estudio   (Another went to study,
virudio, virudio,   stirudy, stirudy,
de pico picotudio   with a mouth, mouthudy,
de pomporirá.   with a pomporira.)

Otro iba al colegio   (The other went to college
viregio, viregio,   collirege, collirege,
de pico picotegio,   with a mouth, mouthege,
de pomporirá.   with a pomporira.)

Aquí termina el cuento   (Here ends the story
viruento, viruento,   sturory, sturory,
de pico picotuento   with a mouth, mouthory,
de pomporirá.   with a pomporira.) *

There will no doubt be those who object to a sexual origin for embolalia, holding rather that it fulfills a rhythmic musical function. This overlooks the fact that rhythm itself has a sexual origin. Ramos takes this position and bases his opinions on those of Germain ("La musique et l'inconscient," *Revue française de psicanalise*, 1928), Alexander Elster (*Musik und Erotik: Betrachtungen zur Sexualsoziologie der Musik*, 1925), and on Freud (*Jenseits des Lustprinzips*, 1923).

NEOLOGISMS

Among the neologisms in folklore we find glossolalia. According to Tanzi it consists of inventing private words and phrases without any rational meaning and filled with emotional values. Glossolalic children are said to undergo illusions when expressing an unspeakable idea with incomprehensible words (63:178, 179). How do we distinguish this from embolalia since the latter is also composed of words and phrases which also do not have rational meaning? In glossolalia the substitution of intellective values of the language by emotional values is complete. One of the most significant popular examples belonging among the children's games is the "foreigner's speech" (63:179).

Is there anyone who doesn't remember playing at "cowboys and Indians" in his childhood, with the unvarying presence of the three central characters of the game: the good guy, the outlaw, and the Indian? The Indian is the glossolalic child of this group. He is the one who "speaks like a foreigner." Some of these forms

*Translator's note: Embolalias are untranslatable. These are only attempts to give an approximate idea.

of speech become at times traditionalized in folklore and Ramos
provides us with one of them as an example:

(19) Patativa chore e lamba,
     Caracá gerecerão
     Cerracarri arritinboque
     Pirepares guatanboque
     Pirispares e parum,
     Cem vêzes pariu marum.
     Quagi-guagé e guagiganga,
     Cocoriágua quiticanga,
     Riticasco e morombêta,
     Tetetererê trombeta
     Patativa chore e lamba (63:180).*

When stereotypes and neologisms are clothed with magical powers, that is, when the language joins the symbolism of oral libido
with narcissism, then these stereotypes and neologisms become
authentic oral fetishes, verbal talismans, and completely miraculous formulas. In case these incantations and sortileges are neither
embololalic or glossolalic, their study must be deferred exclusively
to the classification of narcistic oral libido.

MIMICRY

In certain situations mimicry accompanies or even substitutes for
the spoken language. Embolalias, glossolalias, and verbal formulas
have their corresponding mimicry which is a certain form of oral
libido. "The aggressive components of oral libido are the ones
which are exteriorized in this way with a wealth of gestures,"
Ramos writes, referring to the wealth of mimicry among primitive
people (63:186; 60:402).

In support of his position he cites the statement made by Nina-
Rodrigues concerning the exaggerated mimicry of Afro-Bahians:
"The importance and the role of gesture, action, mimicry, in the
Negro's language is of such an order that without their help he
could only make himself understood with difficulty." Nina-

---

*While these verses have lexical meaning, it is unknown to the children
who use them.

Rodrigues in turn quoted the statement of a traveller from Africa, Dias de Carvalho, in 1890, who related the interpolations of the Lunda language as follows:

(20) The interpolations consist of some special terms, old phrases, suitable interjections, gestures, and movements of the various parts of the body. It is by means of these that they succeed in obtaining the emphasis and exaggeration considered indispensable to obtain the best meaning in their speeches. It is during the *mussumba,* in the presence of the Muatianva, that these interjections are observed the most. They need some of them to substitute for terms which they do not have or which they have forgotten such as the divisions of the day, providing directions, distances, heights, thickness, etc., which are indicated with the arms and hands. Other interjections such as speed, sudden suspension in midair, dangers, precipices, etc., are accomplished by mimicry and special expressions in addition to well-known gestures and movements.

"The hours of the day are shown in the following way: raising the right hand to the zenith means midday; stretching out the latter in the direction the sun rises means six o'clock in the morning; stretching in the other direction (that of the setting sun) means six o'clock in the afternoon. Nine o'clock and three o'clock in the afternoon are estimated by bending the hand in the direction of the angle concerned. Bending them this way they do not differ a great deal from our own divisions of time.

"They express the concept of distances by placing their left hand on their chest and stretching out their right arm and pointing out with their hand more or less in the direction of the place referred to. If they are in this position and at the same time they strike their chests with their left hand, they are indicating the seasons.

Referring to the above quotation from Dias, Nina-Rodrigues concludes: "The survival of this aptitude for thought is exhibited in the garrulity of our population. This interesting confluence of mimicry and the spoken forms of African languages leads us to anticipate that there is a definite influence which causes the exuberance of the unrhythmic mimetic gestures of all cultures. This is plentiful and rich among Brazil's plebeian masses. What is certain, however, is that from it emanates the common practice among the masses of substituting the gesture for the spoken word or at least by producing the former and the latter together consistently" (63:186–189, cf. 53:233).

The oral libido is an extensive and fascinating topic. In this discussion we are only considering its folkloric implications; however, its extra-folkloric applications are extensive. The pronunciation of obviously obscene words with sadistic aggressiveness thus becomes a manifestation of oral libido. Likewise are the length of screams, prattling of children's conversation, the elegant products of modernist poetry which uses infantile pregenital forms, and includes the "use of words with mellifluous, sweet attributes" which mothers use with their children, or sweethearts with each other: sweetheart, honey, sugarplum, snookey, and wookey. Ramos adds: "Regression at times even reaches the stage of baby talk characterized by mimicry and misused labials, especially among women" (63:190–192).

At this point we call attention to a folkloric game which mothers in the northwest of Brazil use to make their children laugh. With their index fingers they tickle their children's noses, chins, and finally their foreheads saying:

(21) Bilu, bilu, bilu, la tête!
      (Coochie, coochie, coochie, cute child!)

In conclusion, we support Ramos' statement that "language does not have as its sole function the communication of thought. It has a primitive, asocial, egotistical objective working with the oral activities of the libido" (63:194).

6

Anal Libido

One of the folkloric manifestations of sadistic anal libido takes root in the strange and sordid scatological therapy of people in rural regions. This filthy plebeian medicine and, in general, certain equally filthy magical practices designed to attract wealth, make up the chapter on folklore which in 1936 Saintyves titled *cabinet secret du folklore* (folklore's secret closet) (67:81).

It is not unusual for us to receive irrelevant and puritanical admonitions on furnishing research data from folklore's secret closet. These admonitions of course come from individuals who are ignorant about our subject and who are incapable of noting the difference between the sexual and the obscene. We feel no compulsion to listen to them. I recall that it was Freud who stated that congeniality and aversion must be left aside when one wishes to penetrate reality (63). If the layman wants to object, he does so without courtesy, in any manner whatever, and with a minimal element of responsibility. Was not this the approach used when they criticized Freud's work, saying that it was no more than an excuse to talk about filth in the living room? (58).

There are no obscenities then in "folklore's secret closet." It is a chapter which respectfully treats the sexual system of folklore such as sexual magic and sexual embolalia. I am referring to ideas which are going to sound bad to certain individuals, ideas which are usually rude expressions; although they are rude in other circumstances, they are not in psychoanalytical folklore.

Among folklore items cited by Ramos in his essay are some

which were copied from a work of Paul Courbon in France and others collected by Ramos himself in Brazil (58:179–180).

(22) Ulcerated hands are cured by bathing them in urine.

(23) Preserving children's dandruff in their hair and never cleaning it under any condition prevents meningitis.

(24) Curing traumatisms either by internal or external application of the "wine of droppings" is done in certain parts of France. It consists of an infusion of dog dung in grape juice.

(25) Horse dung is used as an ointment on wounds.

(26) Pure saliva, or saliva mixed with a little clay, is also used as an ointment.

(27) Stove lampblack is also used as an ointment.

(28) Coffee strained through certain very intimately used garments acquires the miraculous properties of a love philter.

To these examples we could add a countless number of others. Concerning this I recall from my Paraguayan-Brazilian research that:

(29) *Quebra-quebra* tea (well dried dog dung) cures whooping cough in children (11).

(30) Dog's white fecal matter, "sugar of the fields," is good for measles (14).

(31) Prostitute: a. To keep a man and prevent him from loving another, on a Friday she must pour a stewpot of water over her head, catch it between her legs, prepare coffee with it, and give it to the man she loves; b. To keep the man and make him loving again, prepare coffee in the usual way. To this add three drops of menstruation. (Because of this, experienced men neither eat nor drink anything in their houses.) c. Still for the same purpose they pull a hair off their head, one from their sexual organ, and one from each armpit, thus forming a cross in the sexual act. Afterwards they roast them, grind them to make them into powder, and mix them in the man's food or coffee (11).

(32) To regain one's speech, boil cow dung. When cold, strain the infusion and drink it (17).

(33) For illnesses of the urinary tract take *taravé rupiá* tea (cockroach eggs boiled in water). Take out the eggs and drink the liquid (17).

(34) For convulsions (metritis) rub the belly down with sheep grease and bathe with very warm water frequently (17).

(35) To regain one's sense of hearing, the worms in cow dung are gathered up and placed in cotton in the ears (17).

(36) The woman must anoint her body with *Kai guyrá* (monkey grease). This provides her with the affection of others and she will have her lover as she wishes (17).*

HAVELOCK ELLIS' CONTRIBUTION

Without a doubt one of the most important contributions on this topic is that of Havelock Ellis. The famous psychologist labored at it with cold objectivity in his *Sexual Psychology* (22). Studying the various erotic symbols or sexual equivalents he included scatological symbolism among them. He does not derive it from sadistic anal libido but he certainly recognizes it as a sexual symbol, as an erotic symbol. For didactic purposes he classifies it in two subdivisions—the urolagnic and the coprolagnic—according to the ancient proverb: *Inter faeces et urinam nascimur.* Furthermore he points out that Maeder uses the word *koprophilia* to include both urolagnia and coprolagnia (22). Under this classification Ellis studies not only folkloric acts but also sublimated examples in cultured literature unmistakably tied to the scatological group of erotic symbols.

There are many folkloric acts of a urolagnic nature mentioned by Havelock Ellis. He introduces them and classifies them in four groups: urine considered as a primitive holy water; as a possessor of magical properties; as the object of theological folkloric literature. The fourth group includes the acts not included in the other three. The following describe uses of urine as primitive holy water:

(37) It is a custom among the Hottentots for the doctor to urinate alternately on the bride and the groom, and victorious young warriors sprinkle them the same way (22).

(38) Mungo Park says that in Africa on one occasion a bride sent him a cask containing urines which were sprinkled on him as a sign of special honor for an illustrious guest (22).

(39) The highlanders throw urine on their cattle as if it were holy water, the first Monday of each trimester (22).

(40) The women of the Chevsurs, an Iranian people of the Caucasus, after having given birth—a period during which they

---

*Strictly speaking examples (23), (26), (27), (28), (31), (33), (34), and (36), although filthy are not scatological. They are a part of anal libido only by extension and are considered parascatological.

live separated from their husbands—purify themselves in cow urine, then return to their homes. This manner of purification is recommended by the Avesta, and it is said that it is used by the few who are members of this creed (22).

Havelock Ellis states that among many primitive people around the world and among the lower classes of civilized peoples urine possesses magical properties. This appears to be so primarily for the urine of women and for those who have or hope to have sexual relations. For example:

(41) In an Indian legend of northeastern North America, a woman gives her lover some of her urine and says, "You can awaken the dead by putting some drops of my urine in their ears and nose" (22).

(42) There is a legend among the same Indians concerning a woman with beautiful white skin who noted that every morning as she bathed in the river the fishes were attracted by her skin and did not go away even when magic words were spoken. Finally she said to herself, "I will urinate on them, and they will then leave me alone." She did so, and from that time on the fishes left her alone. But soon afterwards the fire from heaven killed her (22).

(43) Among Christians and Mohammedans in Turkey the wife can lure the unfaithful husband by secretly mixing her urine in his drink (22).

Urine appears as an object of theological folkloric literature in the legend of Debforgaill. Havelock Ellis observes that according to J. Rhys in his *Lectures on the Origin and Growth of Religion*, Debforgaill might in reality be the goddess of dusk, the drop which shines beneath the rays of the sun, as indicated by her name which means drop or tear. Ellis relates the legend as it appears in a work by Zimmer.

(44) A certain number of princesses of Emain Macha, the residence of the Kings of Ulster, resolved to find out which one among them could melt a pillar of snow by urinating on it, and thus declare her the best among them. None of them were able to do it and so they sent for Debforgaill who was in love with Cuchullain and she melted the pillar. As a result of this the rest of the women, jealous of the superiority she had demonstrated, put out her eyes (22).

In the fourth group of urological acts selected by Havelock Ellis, a group which we could call miscellaneous, appears the tale about *La princesse qui pisse par dessus les meules* (the princess who pisses on the haystacks) from the folklore of Picardy. Ellis believes this tale to be a variant of the legend of Debforgaill, but he observes that all religious or theological traces have been lost from it:

> (45) This princess had the habit of urinating on haystacks. The king, her father, in order to break her of this habit offered her hand to anyone who could make a haystack so tall she could not urinate on it. Young men offered their services, but she, carrying out her feat, made fun of them. Finally a young man appeared who said that the princess could not do such a thing once she lost her virginity. He seduced her and she became a laughable sight because when she attempted to practice her old habit, she did no more than wet her hose. Consequently the young man married her (22).

Among the examples of coprolagnic folklore are a group of acts selected by Ellis in which animal excrements have been used as sacred things. Ellis has recourse to India's folklore and makes use of Jules Bois' study, *Visions de l'Inde*, to describe the spectacle of the cows of Benares in the temple:

> (46) I put my head through the opening of the stable. It was the largest of the temples, a splendor of precious stone and marble, where the venerable animals came and went. An entire people worshipped them. Sunk in their dark and divine unconsciousness they pay no attention to the worshippers. And they serenely fulfill their animal duties, ruminating over the offerings, drinking water out of copper vessels, and once they are filled they relieve themselves. Then a stercoral and religious madness grips these women with dauntless faces and these venerable men. They fall to their knees, prostrate themselves, eat the excrement and greedily drink the liquid which according to them is sacred and miraculous (22) .

SCATOLOGICAL SYMBOLISM OF GOLD

In addition to the strange and sordid scatological therapy just noted, folkloric examples of sadistic-anal libido, tales and other types of folklore focusing attention on gold and money, are also worth noting. Fondness for money is, of course, tied to the sadistic-anal complex. Ramos states that money, a pot of money, dough, a paper bill, all these are copro symbols. And the monetary complex in the final analysis is nothing more than the anal complex. It is obvious that the scatology of gold and other similar things is but one more chapter in the secret closet of folklore and if it is set apart here, it is solely for the purpose of properly identifying it.

In developing an explanation for gold as a copro symbol, Ramos called upon Freud, Ferenczi, Jones, M. Féré, and others. His explanation follows a path whose successive points of consideration are: (1) excremental matter, (2) mud, (3) sand, (4) small stones, and (5) money.

At first the child plays with his excremental matter. Esthetic feelings, modesty, shame, loathing, and repugnance are developed under the weight of social pressure. These are not sublimated emotions as in the adult but are related to an infantile cause. This cause is prescribed for the child by the sense of smell. He takes it for granted that the adult prevents his playing with the fecal matter because of its bad odor. Consequently, the child seeks as a substitute for fecal matter another substance which resembles it but is odor free. Mud fulfills these conditions and so it becomes the new toy of the child. New disappointments occur, however, because social coercion has not disappeared.

Following the same process the child now undertakes to discover a successor to mud, but one which is dehydrated. He finds the perfect one in sand. Sand is an odorless and dehydrated copro symbol. Ramos states that "Adults caress them now with their protecting good will, and the children are puffed up with pride in the sand, happy at shaping their buildings, digging wells, digging tunnels, erecting castles with little tools, shovels, rakes, and buckets that were given to them. This is one of the most frequently observed activities." And he adds that "The urinary complex also intervenes in this play activity and its ulterior sublimations. Ferenczi also observed that children obtain a great deal of pleasure from filling with water wells that they dig in the sand and they frequently use their urine for this purpose. These children sublimated their tendencies for future building in adult life, for the specialized engineering of dams, dykes, etc." (58:199–200).

The taste for "doughy, humid, bad-smelling substances" soon

disappears. And the "infantile stone age" begins. Ramos writes, "Now is the time for hard dry little stones. He begins to gather little round pebbles, snow white ones, pieces of chalk, colored stones from the beds of small brooks, or sea shells on the beach. Children collect them with extraordinary pleasure, keeping them, hoarding them, as a result of a primitive instinct and unconscious of their possession, their retention. To the stones are soon added artificial objects of all kinds: small pieces of glass, buttons, etc." (58:201).

Through all these connected phases a common exterior trait is observable: collecting. This provides us with the genesis of adult collecting. The normal adult plays like a child, but his coprological tendency is sublimated. He does not collect feces, nor mud, nor sand, nor stones. He collects different things, money for example. There is not the slightest doubt that monetary interests generally pursue the objective realizations of behavior in accordance with the principle of reality. But in the final analysis the essence of the instinct of capitalism must be found far off in the infantile anal-erotic complex. Ramos affirms that the capitalist is a man "with a repressed and sublimated anal eroticism" (58:204, 209).

As Bastide pointed out, let us not forget that this is a topic of psychoanalytical sociology that doubtlessly "the socialists and communists and other believers of Marxism must be particularly fond of: the association of capitalism with anal eroticism. These are consequently the excremental origins of the system they are combatting" (4:158).

But there is one class of collectors of money whose anal libido is not repressed much less sublimated. These are the misers. Their statements of worship of money are clear manifestations of strong regressions of infantile anal libido. Hernesto Hello, quoted by Féré and Ramos, states, "The miser has physical love for the metal. He loves gold and money in and for themselves. He loves them materially. Contact with the metal provides happiness and physical pleasure. He would probably prefer a lesser amount which is known and seen to a larger but invisible quantity. He has already felt the pieces of gold which he possesses and they instill a personal emotion in him" (58:203).

There are certain folkloric acts which are similar to the miser's in that money constitutes the primordial element. How can it be denied that these acts are no more than expressions of anal libido? Freud himself tells us, "In ancient civilizations, in myths, tales, superstitions, unconscious thought, in dreams and neurosis there is a narrowly established relationship between money and excrement" (58:206).

Concerning this matter we find those folkloric tales of the devil who gives gold to his followers, gold which becomes excrement when he disappears. There is also the European superstition which affirms that the discovery of treasure is equivalent to the act of defecating. This is similar to many items in books of proverbs such as the one which calls hemorrhoids "veins of gold," in the German language of the people, *goldene Ader.* Among the many folkloric tales are those referred to by Jones and Laistner called "The Chicken and the Golden Eggs" and a Scandinavian tale in which gold is analogous to hair (the maiden lets pieces of gold fall as she loosens her hair).

To all these examples mentioned by Ramos, I must add three more: the Brazilian student's slang "to be clean" which means to be out of money; Grimm's fairy tale about the giant, the devil, and the three golden hairs; and certain Brazilian versions of Cinderella where the heroine flings diamonds when she speaks.

Unfortunately Ramos does nothing more than point out this folkloric classification since his area of primary concern did not include it. In this volume I have tried to avoid as much as possible this defect. For this reason therefore I am including a version of one of the previously mentioned fables:

(47) The Chicken with the Golden Eggs.
Impatient John discovered a hen laying eggs of gold behind his house. But she laid only one per week. Filled with happiness he told his wife: "We are rich! This chicken has a treasury in its ovaries, I will kill it and become the leader of the territory."

"Why should you kill it, when by keeping it you get an egg of gold every week?"

"They don't call me Impatient John for nothing! Do you want me to be satisfied with an egg a week when I can get a hold of the entire nestful in an instant?"

And he killed the chicken.

Inside it there was only guts like in ordinary hens and Impatient John, flouted and mocked, continued marking time his whole life and died penniless (53:159).

I would also like to add the renowned version of "The Lazy One" from Morro das Pedras in Belo Horizonte, Brazil:

(48) The Lazy One or The Ass that Defecated Gold*

There was once a very poor and very lazy man who had a great many children. His wife constantly sent him out to work. Many times he went out to work but found no work or when he found some it did not work out well. Nothing ever worked out well.

One day he took his axe and went to the woods to cut some firewood. He walked and arrived in the woods very tired. He sat down, rested a bit, and then began to cut firewood. He had already made the chips fly quite a bit when the axe flew out of his hand and fell into a well. Then he, very sad, without knowing what he was doing, sat in the shade at the edge of the well and began to think about what was to become of him if he arrived home without the firewood and the axe. He would get another beating from his wife! Then he became even sadder. He immediately heard a voice saying, "Put your hand in the well and you will get a surprise." But he was frightened and did not do so. Then he heard the voice again. And again he did not put his hand in it. The voice came again a third time repeating the same thing: "Put your hand in the well." When he put his hand in the well he was puzzled to find, instead of the axe, a tablecloth. He stood there like a dolt with the tablecloth in his hands without knowing what to do because what he wanted was the axe to take home. Immediately he heard the same voice telling him: "This tablecloth is charmed; when you want to eat you only have to say: 'Tablecloth, set the table!' and a table full of rich food, the best things that you can imagine, will appear." And he stood there somewhat doltishly refusing to believe. At the same time since he was very hungry he said to try it out: "Tablecloth, set the table!" And the tablecloth set out a meal of the best things. He was astounded and ate his fill. Afterwards he said the opposite words, "Tablecloth, clear the table!" And the meal and the table disappeared and the tablecloth became again only a tablecloth.

Joyfully he folded the tablecloth, put it in his pocket and gave thanks to God and hurried home because he remembered that his family was alone and hungry. But it took him a long time to arrive home. He had to cross many fields and sleep along the way. Along the road there was an old woman's shack. He reached it and asked for shelter so as to spend a night there. The old woman said yes that he could come in. He said that as payment for her hospitality he was going to have a meal prepared for them to eat. The old woman was an evil witch and she was crazy about the tablecloth. After finishing the meal she made a bed for him and said, "This is

*This is the same as "El burro que caga plata," by Susana Chertudi, *Cuentos folklóricos argentinos* (1960).

for you to sleep on." Since he was very tired he went to bed and slept deeply without worrying about the tablecloth. Taking advantage of his sleep the witch took another tablecloth, stole his, and placed the other one in its place. The man got up in the morning, thanked the old woman a great deal, took the tablecloth, put it in his pocket, and set out for home.

When he was arriving home he saw his wife and children from a distance. He raised the tablecloth in the air and began to wave it saying, "Woman, I have a surprise for you! Come and see this wonderful thing! Now we will never be hungry again. God has had pity on us!" He reached home and all his children surrounded him and stretched the tablecloth out on the ground. The woman who was always against him began to prattle: "Let's see what kind of a surprise you have. Instead of looking for work you look for children's games." But they all stood curiously around the tablecloth. Then he said, "Tablecloth, set the table!" and the tablecloth did nothing at all. He was very surprised and repeated the same words again. He said the same words three times and the tablecloth did not set the table. The wife became terribly angry. She picked up a stick and gave the man a terrible beating saying, "Get to work you begging dog! Instead of looking for work you set out to find fables."

Very sad because of what had happened he picked up an axe and went to the same place to cut firewood. While he was cutting firewood the axe fell behind a group of shrubs. Then he heard the same words. "Look behind the shrubs and you will find a surprise." He moved in a hurry because of his first experience. And he thought that he would find the tablecloth there. But he did not find it. He found an ass grazing. He paid no attention to the ass but continued to look for the tablecloth thinking that he would find it again. Then he heard the same voice saying, "This ass defecates money. You only have to say: 'Ass, make ready!'" To try it out, he said: "Ass, make ready!" And the ass began to defecate money. He filled his pockets, filled his hat, filled everything with money. When he saw that he had no place left to put money he laid hold of the ass and set out for home.

He stopped at the house of the same old woman and asked for shelter. While talking, he told the old woman that the ass defecated gold, that God had had pity on him, and that he did not know what had happened to his tablecloth. Then the old woman said, "Ah my son, let me see if it is true!" And very ingenuously he ordered the ass to defecate money. Then he sent the ass to retire, and he lay down and slept. The old woman took advantage of his sleeping and did the same thing she had done with the tablecloth. She brought another ass, tied it in the same place, and took his ass, the real one and hid it. In the morning he did the same thing, he got up, took his ass, thanked the old woman, took his leave and set out for home.

When he arrived home the woman saw him from a distance. Very happily he cried out: "Oh woman, I am bringing an ass! You are going to see what a beauty it is, what a surprise it has in store for you!" She said, "Yes you are coming here with an ass to dirty my patio. In addition to not helping me, you are hindering me." He took the ass and put it in the middle of the lot and said: "Ass, make ready!" Then the ass began to defecate real dung. He was very perplexed and the woman was indignant. She picked up a stick and gave him a beating. And she sent him back to the woods and told him not to come home again.

He went back to the same place hoping to find the things he had lost because he had a great deal of faith in God and he prayed a great deal. When he began to cut the firewood the axe fell in the well as it had the first time. He heard the same voice and put his hand in the well and was startled because he did not take a tablecloth or an ass out of it. He pulled out a small club similar to any other piece of wood. He heard the same voice. "This little club will be very useful to you. You will never again be beaten and you will now be able to boss everyone who bosses you about. You will be able to get everything you want. You only have to say 'Little club, do your duty!' and it will give a whipping to anyone around." And the voice continued, saying: "Go to the house of the old woman where you slept. That old woman is a witch. Tell her to give you your things because she has them all hidden. She is going to deny this, but tell your little club to do its duty until she turns everything over to you. After she has turned everything over to you, order the little club to stop."

He took the little club and went to the old woman's house. When he arrived at the old lady's house he asked her to return everything to him. He said, "I want my tablecloth and my ass." And the old woman refused, saying, "But my son, I am a poor old woman, and you think that I would steal something from you." Then he said, "Little club, do your duty!" The little club then began to beat the old woman on the face, on the legs, everywhere. All the while the old woman screamed, "Stop, my son! Stop, for the love of God!" Then he said, "I will only stop after you have returned my things to me." The old woman ran and got the ass and the tablecloth and returned them. Then he ordered the little club to stop. He checked to see if it was really his tablecloth and if it was really his ass and set out for home.

On arriving home his wife saw him coming from a distance and she began to shout, "Are you coming again with another ass?" And she began to threaten him, "This time I am going to break your bones." Even their children were by now accustomed to the mother threatening the father with beatings and even helping the mother beat the father. Then he said, "This time I have a tremendous surprise for you, you will see." But the mother couldn't care less, and she picked up a stick and waited for him, stick in hand. When he arrived the first thing he did was to say, "Little club, do your duty!" The little club jumped and began to whip the mother and children. They cried out, "Stop, for the love of God! I can't stand it any more! We'll never hit you again!" As soon as he saw that they could stand no more he ordered the little club to stop. Then he stretched out the tablecloth and it set out a meal for everyone, food, sweets, the best of everything they could think of. When they had all eaten their fill, he ordered the tablecloth to collect itself. Afterwards he said: "That is nothing, woman, you are now going to see my little ass which defecates gold. We are going to be the richest people in the world." And he said: "Little ass! Make ready!" And the little ass began to defecate gold. The woman and the children were astounded by this and began to ask how he had gotten all these things. And he related how everything had happened and lived happily and rich for the rest of his life (11).

The fairy tale "The Little Girl with the Gold Earrings" collected by Nina-Rodrigues in Bahia is also very suggestive (53:286). Câmara Cascudo included it in his anthology *Contos tradicionais do Brasil* and provided interesting annotations showing how, for example, "excrement" is replaced by "filth" in other versions ("O surrão" in the Portuguese version); by a cat and a dog ("El zurrón que cantaba" in the Spanish version); by a chamber pot ("O Negro do surrão" or "A moça do surrão" in Brazil); by a raven ("Sigô," in one African version), or by snakes and toads ("The Story of the Cannibal's Wonderful Bird," in another African version) (5:169–170).

(49) The Girl with the Golden Earrings

A mother who was very strict with her children gave her little daughter some gold earrings as a present. When the child went to the fountain to fetch water and to take a bath she was in the habit of taking off her earrings and putting them on a stone.

One day she went to the fountain, filled the gourd and returned home, forgetting the earrings. Arriving home she missed them, and, afraid that her mother would tear her to pieces and punish her, she ran back to the fountain to find the earrings. Arriving there she found a very old man who grabbed her, put her on his shoulders, and carried her away with him. The old man held the girl, put her in a big sack, sewed the sack up and told the girl he would go with her from door to door to earn his living, and when he would tell her to she should sing while inside the bag. If she did not do so he would hit her with his cane. Everywhere he went he threw the sack on the ground and said:

> Sing my sack.
> If you do not
> I'll whip you with my cane.

And the sack sang:

> They put me in this sack
> And I'm bound to die
> In this sack,
> Because of some gold earrings
> That I lost at the fountain.

Everyone was amazed and gave the old man some money. On a certain day he arrived at the house of the girl's mother, and she recognized her daughter's voice. She then invited the old man to eat and drink, and since it was already late, they strongly urged him to stay and sleep. At night he slept very soundly since he had drunk more than his fill. The mother went and opened the sack and took out the little girl who was exhausted and almost dead. In place of the child, they filled the sack with excrement.

The following day, the old man woke up, grabbed his sack, put it on his shoulder and went on his way. At a house further down the road he asked if they wanted to hear his sack sing. He placed the sack on the ground and said:

> Sing, sing my sack.
> If you do not
> I'll whip you with my cane.

Nothing. The sack was silent. He said it again, and still nothing. Then the old man struck the sack; it split open and revealed the trick the mother had played on the old man. He was enraged.

Among other examples of scatological gold we should also note the Paraguayan superstition according to which:

(50) Invountarily stepping in excrement is an omen of money (17).

And in Uruguay:

(51) To dream about money means a louse and vice versa (16).

We should also note Jung's comment. After stating that there exists an intimate relationship between feces and gold, he says that the most valueless thing is associated with the most valuable one. To support his statement he wrote:

(52) Basing his notion on folklore, De Gubernatis states that feces have always been associated with gold. On the basis of his

psychological experience Freud says the same thing. Grimm makes reference to the following magical practice: "If you want to have gold at home the whole year long you must eat lentils on New Year's Day." This unusual relationship is explained simply by the physiological reality of the difficulty of digesting lentils, which are very frequently evacuated in the shape of coins. Thus one transforms one's self into an evacuator of gold (44:202).

Finally here is an act which I cannot overlook and whose inclusion in the chapter on scatological folklore has preoccupied me. It deals with the feast of Saint Conon. It was studied in a separate monograph after field research conducted in the city of Florida, Uruguay, in June 1954. But I wish here to add an analytical demopsychological interpretation to it.

> (53) Saint Conon is a saint brought from Italy and he is revered in the city of Florida without the clergy's approval. His sect is controlled by a governing board of descendents of old Italian colonists. Saint Conon's day, the third of June, attracts a remarkable crowd from several parts of the Republic. Notes and hundred peso bills adorn the saint's pockets, rings cover his fingers, the ex-votos— hearts, legs, arms, etc.,—minted in gold and other metals also cover his habit or fill showcases scattered throughout the chapel. At the same time a lively commerce has grown in front of the chapel and countless gold or golden trinkets are sold. In addition lottery tickets are sold. There are many lottery ticket sellers with their typical cries who hawk their wares up and down the street (12).

What can the cult of this saint offer scatological folklore? Precisely the fact that the cult is characterized, above all, by offerings of money, gold, metal. We could say that Saint Conon's chapel is not a chapel but a bank because of the incalculable fortune of offerings it contains. The topic becomes more interesting on observing that the surroundings are a money complex.

Apparently the explanation offered concerning Saint Conon's association with money results from luck at the lottery. His number, 3 (3 is a sexual symbol), has the luck of always being drawn in the game. The one who offers pious vows and gambles with faith in Saint Conon gives him a percentage of his winnings if he is successful. They even make crosses out of money. Could there not be among his worshippers those who by extension worship the money which covers his body? Of course this is so! The world is full of misers, of those who worship money because of its form, its color, its strange fascination.

It is very possible that the worship of Saint Conon by extension transforms itself into a money cult, if it has not already unconsciously done so. The saint can remain hidden to the eyes of many believers even though possibly when they turn their faces up to him they see nothing more than the valuables on his habit. In conclusion, according to analytical demopsychology the cult of Saint Conon is very possibly an example of the anal-sadistic libido. It is said that these are cultures whose social character has a cumulative (anal) orientation while others have a receptive (oral) orientation (68:28). The social character of Saint Conon's cult appears to have an accumulative-retentive (anal) orientation. This could stem from infantile anal frustrations.

Additional support is provided this hypothesis when we note that a conflict developed when a new Saint Conon was brought from Italy. The apparent objective was to damage the reputation of the original Saint Conon. The devotees kept the statue in the chapel since it was the genuine one. Unconsciously they preferred the statue with money that shone on its cloak and they called the new Saint Conon "counterfeit." Note that "genuine" and "counterfeit" are purely economic concepts. The cathedral will some day embellish its new Saint Conon with jewels, gold, and banknotes and it will then be possible to disperse the endless mass of believers at the original Saint Conon's chapel. This is true because the motive for this worship is a frankly anal-sadistic regression.

SCATOLOGICAL SYMBOLISM OF PURIFICATION RITES

In folklore there is another class of acts originating from anal libido. These are those which contain the exact opposite idea, that of purification. "The ideas of *pure* and *impure*, that is, of dirty and clean, reflect the success of censorship over primitive concern for coprological elements," writes Ramos. And he adds, "It is from these that the symbolic ideas of rituals of purification—which, let us note in passing, are very common among savages in certain folklore customs and primarily in religions—are closely related to anal-rectal concerns and the subsequent ideas of filth and impurity. The purification ceremony is a maximum attempt at freedom from the anal-rectal complex. It is an unconscious effort at sublimation on the road to the glorious conquest of the pure, the transparent, the clean, the immaculate in the *élan* of the religious soul" (58:213).

Psychoanalytically the following purification ceremony in the *candomblés* (variants of voodoo rites) of Bahia, Brazil, which is cited from among those collected by Carneiro can be considered the sublimated expression of anal-erotic impulses:

> (54) On a certain Friday the feast of the water of Oxalá is celebrated in all the *candomblés*. In the old Sugar Plantation this ceremony is celebrated the last Friday in August and in Opô Afonjá of Aninha on the last Friday of September. During the first hours of the morning, when it is still dark, the daughters, dressed completely in white, go in a procession to the fountain which serves the *candomblé*. They carry earthenware jugs, pitchers, porous clay water jugs, small water jugs, and other clay receptacles while singing canticles and dancing. They carry water into the ceremonial house to renew it. Meanwhile the great drums are beating; the girls enter in single file with their receptacles on their shoulders, going back and forth over the path between the ceremonial house and the fountain under the hesitant light of dawn. This same day, at nighttime, the *candomblé* has a festival (8:69).

On the other hand, we must not forget that purification stems from the concept of taboo. If the taboo is violated, the individual is induced to purify himself. The most common act of the immaculate superego on the "sinning" ego is obsessive ablution, as Freud observes (34:434).

NON-FOLKLORIC SCATOLOGY

The manifestations of anal-sadistic libido exist also outside of our field of specialization. There are, for example, the taste for perfumes, the "flatus-complex" mentioned by Jones, the inclination for the spreading of certain ideas, and the belief in telepathy. The topic has been researched to such an extreme, either correctly or incorrectly, that even characterological types related to the anal-erotic complex have been outlined.

We are not basically interested in such extra-folkloric manifestations. Those who wish to become acquainted with them in detail should refer to Ramos' "A sordície nos alienados e o complexo anal-erótico" (58) and Havelock Ellis' previously cited *Psychology of Sex* (22).

In conclusion we believe that folkloric expressions from the secret closet of folklore as well as certain items on gold and mystical purification ceremonies may well be, as Ramos suggests, the work of a folk impelled "by a fundamental impulse which was discovered by psychoanalysts after groping and dilatory effects" (58:219).

7

Genital Libido and Narcissism

Neither Ramos nor anyone else that I know of has until now considered the folkloric expressions of genital libido. Neverthless its existence cannot be doubted. The genital phase brings to a close the libido's developmental cycle. In it the individual projects himself toward an exterior sexual object. It is therefore logical that plebeian acts which make mention of the phallus, the vagina, and the perverted anus be recognized as bound to this phase, and these are numberless.

In my *Folklore y Educación* I cite a complete list of these from which the following examples have been selected:

(55)	—Diz machado!	—(Say tass!
	—Machado!	—Tass!
	—Teu cu está inchado.	—You have a swollen ass.)
		(From Brazilian folklore)
(56)	Metío, metío	(He put it, he put it,
	en el poto de tu tío.	in your uncle's ass.)
		(From Chilean folklore.)
(57)	Dos contra uno	(Two against one—
	Le meten la paja en er cu. .	They stuff the straw up his a . .)
		(From Spanish folklore)

MAGIC

Magic is one of the most obvious folkloric manifestations of narcissism. Freud uses the expression omnipotence of ideas (*Allmacht der Gedanken*) to explain it psychoanalytically. This was prompted by one of his patients during treatment. Freud noted that this patient suffered from obsessive representations. "It was enough for him to think about a person for him to meet him at once as if he had conjured him up. If one day he would happen to ask for news of an individual that he had lost sight of for some time, it would be to find out that he had just died. It could therefore be felt that this person had telepathically attracted his attention. When without any bad intention whatever he would curse anyone at all, he lived from that moment on in perpetual fear of finding out the death of that person and perishing under the weight of the responsibility incurred" (34:465). This patient called the power of his own ideas over the exterior world the omnipotence of ideas.

The frame of reference is very similar to the magic of the primitive or the plebeian, and because of this Freud adopted this illustrative expression. The savage, the plebeian, the child, and the neurotic believe "they can transform the exterior world with their ideas alone," and that because of this they are "omnipotent." It can be clearly seen that this omnipotence of ideas in and of itself involves a supervaluation of the ego, a personal overestimation. In other words, it has a narcissistic foundation. As narcissism is an autoerotic consequence, it can be deduced that the omnipotence of ideas is basically a strongly sexualized thought. Magic is then a sexual phenomena. Sexual magic could be considered pleonasm.

The examples cited by Freud are rather significant. For example, he cites magic acts to hurt an enemy, to cause rain, and to achieve a good harvest. Among magical practices to hurt an enemy one of the most frequently used

(58) consists of building his effigy out of any kind of materials and without his resemblance being an essential factor. It is even possible to state that any object at all is this effigy. Everything that is inflicted on it will befall the individual it represents. It is sufficient to wound a part of the former for the corresponding organ of the latter to become sick" (34:461).

Among the methods for attracting rain is the following from the Ainu of Japan:

(59) Citing Frazer, Freud writes that the Japanese Ainu believe they cause rain by pouring water through a large fishing net and

carrying through the village a large canoe equipped with a sail and oars as if it were a ship.

On the other hand, Freud adds that the fertility of the land is magically assured by offering a pageant of sexual relations. The following example from Java is very illustrative:

(60) In certain regions of the islands of Java, when the time for the rice to bloom approaches, the men and women workers go to the fields at night so as to stimulate, by their example, the ground's fertility, thus guaranteeing a good crop (34:462).

This omnipotence of course requires one principal condition for its realization: faith. It must be believed that ideas can be omnipotent. The magician, the animist, the religious of all faiths admit that their ideas do not become omnipotent if they are not believed capable of it. Freud states that they admit "that it is useless to invoke the spirits if one does not have faith, and that the magical strength of prayer remains ineffective if it is not inspired by true piety."

Freud illustrates this with the passage from Hamlet when King Claudius exclaims: "My words ascend. My thoughts remain below. Words without ideas never reach heaven" (34:464–465). The same thing was said in different words by Doña Maria dos Pintados, the sorceress informant from Morro das Pedras, who when queried on the value of her "blessing," answered that one only needed to have faith. "It is nonsense to bless without faith," she added (14).

I have no doubt that the concept of the omnipotence of ideas advanced by Freud corrects and amplifies Lévy-Bruhl's law of participation, as well as animism first dealt with by Tylor. Tylor's animism, Lévy-Bruhl's law of participation, and Freud's omnipotence of ideas are three major pillars in studies of primitive mentalities of plebeians (the *vulgo* in Spanish of *folk*-lore).

Freud provides us not only with the concept of magic but with a system for its classification. He adopts Frazer's noted outline of contagious magic and imitative magic or homeopathy. A common characteristic of both is that of being telepathic. This means that real distance means nothing in the magic act. What counts above all is the omnipotence of ideas.

Nevertheless, they are different because contagious magic requires a certain "spatial relationship, that is, contiguity and its representation or recollection" (practices to hurt an enemy). Imitative magic in turn requires a certain "analogy between the act performed and the production of the desired phenomena." "If we want it to rain," states Freud, "we will have to do something which imitates or recalls rain." As a basis for his evolutionist concept he adds, "In a phase of more advanced civilization this magical procedure is replaced by processions around a temple and supplications to the saints venerated in it. And further advanced yet, this religious technique will also be replaced by attempts to discover by means of what actions on the atmosphere itself it is possible to induce rain" (34:463). The spatial relationship and analogy mentioned constitute fundamentally two additional conditions for the fulfillment of the omnipotence of ideas. As we noted the first one was faith.

When it is complex, almost all magic is accompanied by dances, music, and songs. These are procedures that are also bound to narcissism and the omnipotence of ideas, and when practiced, assist the effectiveness of the magic. In other words they evoke magic, they are "processes for magical reinforcement," according to Arthur Ramos (60:XIV).

He supports his ideas with those of Reik, who says, "The entire magical-religious ritual dance is a representation of the movements of dead gods, the father-totem. As music it is an imitation of their voices. The erotic in primitive dances becomes transformed with cultural evolution, until it originated the esthetic sublimations of civilized dances." "In effect," Ramos states, "in Brazil's *candomblés* and *macumbas* (variants of voodoo rites) the dance is stylized to promote the *conditions of sainthood*, which from the psychoanalytical point of view expresses the complete erotization of the body, the same as the hysterical seizure which symbolizes coitus" (60:396–397).

The erotic character of primitive dances, in Ramos' opinion, recorded by so many ethnographers, is not an obscene phenomenon as is frequently implied, but a sexual one. It is profoundly sincere, normal, and coherent. The sexual appears "as a force instinctively inherent in their personality, a force of magic and power, and without the deformations and hard meanings attributed to it by civilized mentalities, the captive of untold pressures" (60:396, 398).

GEZA ROHEIM: WITCHES

Once the field of the psychoanalysis of primitive man began to be explored there was no lack of students. Géza Roheim, a specialist in magic, was one of these. His contribution was the psychoanalysis of witches. He felt that witches devolved from narcissism which was clarified by the concept of the overvaluation of the power of thought. Ramos clarified his point of view as follows:

(a) In magical practices the sorcerer is the representative of the phallic power of generation of the group. He retains the vital element and governs it at his pleasure. He projects his phallic power from a distance.

(b) His libido (the sorcerer's) does not have only one narcissistic manifestation. This being so, *mana* comes from an identification with the primitive father. The one who keeps the *mana* in reality hoards the paternal phallus and in this way identifies himself with the father.

(c) Evil witchcraft is a symbolic castration accomplished by the sorcerer, the keeper of paternal (phallic) power. If the human body symbolizes the phallus, the loss of any part of it means castration. When the sorcerer takes possession of a part of the human body—hair, fingernails, excrement, etc.—or destroys it, he performs an aggressive act, a form of castration on the person in question.

(d) Everything about the sorcerer is a symbol of his magical powers. As we have seen, his very body is a phallic symbol. His clothing, his adornment (decorations, taboo, etc.) and his disguises (the use of masks, etc.) are likewise symbolic. His staff, his conjuring brooms and cures for chasing away demons are all symbols of the phallus. Ramos also calls attention to the fact that the hair and the head are primarily and by extension head trophies. To support his interpretation he reasons that if magic is, in the final analysis, an erotic function in the psychoanalytical sense, the body and all its parts are sexual symbols. The *floating libido* can then eroticize any organ as well as any part of the body, even its outer dress (60:394–395).

For additional data on this topic he recommends the reading of Roheim, *Animism, Magic and the Divine King* (1930); "La psychologie raciale et les origines du capitalisme chez les primitifs," *Revue Française de Psychoanalyse* (1929); "Animism and Religion," *The Psychoanalytical Quarterly* (1932); "La psychologie de la zone de culture de l'Australie Centrale," *Revue Française de Psychoanalyse* (1932); "Psychoanalysis of Primitive Cultural

Types," Roheim Australasian Research Number, *International Journal of Psychoanalysis* (1932).

LATIN AMERICAN MAGIC

Examples of folklore magic are numerous in America. The quantity of sources on this topic astound one when we thumb through a bibliography on this topic. Among the many items I collected in Asuncion are the following ones on contagious magic:

(61) If the husband becomes estranged, one must take a used sock, on a Friday, without his noticing it, and then write his name seven times on a piece of paper. The sock must be wrapped in the piece of paper and buried under the threshold. A candle is then lit with its wick down. The husband will soon then return to the right path (17).

(62) When the husband is stubbornly running around with other women his handkerchief is taken from him. It is placed in the brassiere over the breast for three Tuesdays and four Fridays and slept with. The handkerchief is burned at the end of this time and a powder is made from its ashes which is then mixed with perfume. The woman must put this perfume on her face and arms when she goes to bed. She cuddles her husband's head on her arm. She also puts perfume on her husband's clothes when he goes out. In this way the husband and wife fall in love again and he will forget the others (17).

(63) When a husband is stubbornly running around a little of his hair is taken from him. His name is written seven times on a piece of paper, and the hair is wrapped up in the paper with the writing on it. It is placed under Saint Michael's foot and a candle is lit for Saint Michael. Another candle is lit on the floor, this one upside down for the devil (17).

The following are examples of imitative magic:

(64) The pregnant mother must drink water with bluing in it for the baby to have blue eyes (17).

(65) The mother must drink "firewater" for the baby to be born white (17).

When Ramos treated Brazilian magic from the psychoanalytical point of view, he did it primarily in *O Negro brasileiro* in which more than one chapter is dedicated to magic practices and the magic cycle or the psychoanalysis of prelogical thought. In studying these matters Ramos provided greater breadth to Frazer's classifications and put them in tune with Afro-Brazilian reality. He began by adopting an expression by which the savages themselves acknowledge what Freud refers to as the omnipotence of ideas. This expression is *mana*, which according to Lévy-Bruhl was first recorded by Codrington. There are thus those who have more mana or magical powers than others and who are able to extend it to objects. This provides for the conception of fetish objects. Ramos states that those who have greater mystical strength or mana are precisely those who are most powerful: the clergy, the witch doctors, the medicine men (60:391, 392).

Ramos' system for the classification of magic stems from this, and is based on the degree to which the individual possesses greater or lesser mana. This means that they have more or less talent for the omnipotence of ideas according to the objectives for which used. The word clergyman is applied to those who have mana and invoke it for good things. In Brazil the word sorcerer denotes the possessor of mana used for evil. "He has covenants with evil spirits and uses magic processes to cause damage to the group." (60:190) Ramos indicates that these Brazilian sorcerers are the same as the *ñáñigos* of Cuba.* They are also similar to the *payé* of Paraguay.

In giving examples of sorcerers Ramos adopts the subdivisions recommended by Nina-Rodrigues who recognized the practice of two distinct kinds of sorcery: direct or material sorcery, and the indirect or symbolic kind.

The direct one "consists of the direct provision of substances which are poisonous and harmful to the body. For the credulous Negro these are substances possessing only a magic power responsible for its malicious actions." Ramos adds, "Direct sorcery would be a trite chapter of criminology if it were not accompanied by magical and fetishist rituals which provide it with its own *cachet*" (60:192).

Folklore and the history of Brazil are filled with cases of sorcery by poisoning used by black slaves against their white masters. At this time these poisons from the flora and their physiological effects

---

*Among the many works on this topic Fernando Ortiz' *La "tragedia" de los ñáñigos* is recommended (54)

are now better known. The principal raw materials used were *pipi* or *tipi* which is garlic guineahen weed, known also as "guinea weed" (*petiveria aliacea*); *plumbago scandense* or loco weed; *Solanum nigrum*, Moorish herb or animal herb; *acacia farnesiana*, a spongelike herb; and *Xanthosoma sugittaefolium* or elephant's ear taro. Among the substances which "although non-poisonous produce varied reactions and because of this are used in the cult's ceremonies and the practice of sorcery is *Cannabis sativa* or marijuana. The latter comes from Africa where it is known as *liamba, riamba, diamba, pango,* or Angola tobacco" (60:196).

Symbolic magic, on the other hand, is magic proper. (60:207) We must not forget Frazer's already well-known classification of contagious magic (based on the idea of contact) and imitative magic (based on similarity). "Envelopment" is a classic example of imitative Brazilian magic. It corresponds in my opinion to the famous "binding" of Montevidean folklore:

> (66) These are two dolls made of ordinary wool and filled with white rags, about twenty-three centimeters long, and bound together facing each other. They are well fastened by their arms and legs.

An example of contagious and imitative magic occurring simultaneously is the dispatch or *ébó*. It is imitative because it is accomplished by imitation of what is hoped will happen to the person against whom it is directed (for example, a shroud symbolizing death). It is contagious because objects are utilized in it which have either a direct or an indirect relationship with the person in question (60:208). There are various kinds of dispatches and for a variety of purposes. The *effifá*, the *mantucá*, and the *xuxu-guruxú* have all three been observed and documented.

> (67) The xuxu-guruxú is performed with a thorn of St. Anthony's which has been annointed with egg. It is buried in the enemy's doorway. One who wants to inflict harm knocks on the door three times while repeating: "Xuxu-guruxú io le bará."

In Brazil there exists a third category of people who have mana. In addition to the clergyman and the sorcerer there is the medicaster. Ramos points out clearly the difference between a medicaster and a sorcerer, a difference which does not exist in Africa where the sorcerer formerly united his specific activities with those of the group's medicine man. He recommends the adoption of Maxwell's classification in *La Magie* (1933) for the study of Brazilian medicastering. This is:

1. Divinatory medicine (the practice of diagnosis and the search for a remedy).
2. Talismanic medicine (preventatives by means of talismen).
3. Sympathetic medicine (therapeutic magic) (60:213).

Talismanic medicine must be observed carefully. Its principle is essentially fetishist. The holder of mana (the omnipotence of ideas) transmits some of his power to inanimate objects. These objects become fetishes. In Brazil examples of the folk-magic medicine are known under such names as *rezas, garrafadas, banhos de fôlha,* and *mesas.*

ANIMISM AND RELIGION

According to Freud we pass from magic to animism, from animism to religion and from the latter to science. These are phylogenetic and ontogenetic stages. Without a doubt there may be a certain evolutionist concern here but it is very useful for us in attempting to establish a more or less clear and necessary distinction between magic, animism, and religion. They are confused by almost everyone since they are permeated with the principle of the omnipotence of ideas. They are differentiated by a greater or lesser degree of this principle.

Magic utilizes the omnipotence of ideas in its totality, according to Freud. On the other hand, animism cedes a portion of this omnipotence to the spirits. In religion man cedes the omnipotence of his ideas to the gods. Freud explains that he cedes it to the gods without seriously renouncing it in any way since he retains the power of influencing the gods so as to make them act in accordance with his wishes. At the same time in the scientific conception of the world there does not yet exist a place for the omnipotence of man. He has recognized his insignificance, resigned himself to death, and complied with all the remaining natural wants. In our confidence in the power of human intelligence, which deals with the laws of reality, we still find traces of the ancient faith in omnipotence. (34)

The magic, animistic, and religious phases of man are therefore, all of them, to a greater or lesser degree, narcistic phases, that is, phases with a sexual foundation. They respond to an introjection of the libido. The various beliefs related to magic, animism, and religion are therefore narcistic beliefs. The belief in the immortality of the soul, for example, is such a belief. In the effort of conceiving its inaccessibility, its endlessness, its survivance of everything and everyone, man unfolds his personality. He believes himself dual, one who in fact dies, and one who lives on. This alter-ego, identified by the shadow, the reflection, the soul, is the projection of one who loves himself a great deal, of one who enjoys perceptible, indefinable pleasures in his own self. Or at least it may be one who wants to do so, doing so physically either consciously or unconsciously.

In practice these magic, animistic and religious systems have to struggle against the evidence of more enlightened truths. We saw this when I explained Lévy-Bruhl in *The Concept of Folklore* (15). The prelogical mentality prefers to continue being prelogical in spite of objective experience. The persistence of this blindness to the truth of things is evident in the prelogical, magical, animistic, and religious mentality. It is evident in obsessive neuroses also. Obsessive neurotics persist in their representations, in spite of their deeply fixed convictions (34).

In his struggle against evidence to the contrary and to justify his conduct to himself, the magical, animistic, and religious mentality embraces what Freud labels superstition. Freud states that under the control of an animistic system every prescription and every activity must offer a systematic justification which we will label superstition. Superstition like anxiety, dreams, or the devil is one of those temporary structures which collapse under the weight of psychoanalytical research. Moving aside these structures which act like a screen between actions and knowledge we find that the truth and worth of the psychic and cultural life of savages is really quite far from having been appraised (34). Gustave Le Bon in his *L'homme et les sociétés* on the other hand preferred to state that religions express illusions which have been formulated as doctrines (47:II, 183).

The following examples from Brazilian folklore were contributed by Arthur Ramos:

(68) The *ogum* is a ceremony for evoking souls. "The souls which are called out reply to questions, resolve problems, cure sick people. . . . This is what the believers in spiritualism do in their seances today" (60:211).

(69) Funeral rites may also have their origin in the primitive belief in the dual existence of the ego: the ego and the alter ego (animism). "The deceased (the alter ego) exact obligations as if they were alive. The first of these obligations are the funeral rites which are used by all primitive groups" (60:211).

(70) The funeral *candomblé* is a feast celebrated on the cult's property at the death of a Negro member of the sect. There are dances and animal sacrifices in honor of the soul of the dead person and the guardian saints (60:212).

(71) The wake, so well-known in northeastern Brazil for mounting a guard over the deceased, is accompanied by drinking bouts, cries, animated conversation, and laughing (60:212).

(72) The veneration of the twins is, in other words, the veneration of Cosmos and Damian, or the veneration of *Dois-Dois* (The Double Two), the veneration of The Children, which occurs on September 27 according to the folkloric calendar of Bahia (60:378).

Ramos dedicates an entire chapter to the psychoanalytical interpretation of the worship of the twins. He treats it first ethnographically and records its canticles, its food, its practices, its variants. It is the same thing as the worship of the *Jimaguas* in Cuba.

Psychoanalytically it is the expression of the narcistic libido which sees in the alter ego a reflection of the perishable ego, one which we wish to keep from perishing *in aeternum*. "The aspiration to immortality is . . . a chapter of narcistic psychology" (60:388).

Ramos later studies these theories so as to use them as the conclusion of an examination thesis presented for the chair of anthropology and ethnography of the University of Brazil. Although it was attacked, no one was able to destroy its tone of revolutionary originality. Although he was taking an examination which was of crucial importance to his career, it appeared to him that he should advance an idea which was possibly new. In this he struggled daringly against the slow and conservative character of classical Brazilian anthropology.

His thesis, *A organização dual entre os índios brasileiros*, as its title indicates, studies the cultural dualism of various Brazilian indigenous groups. It analyzes the incidence of halves, of doubles, of the number two, be it in family relationships, in religious ceremonies, in work, in recreation, and even in mythology. Because of it Ramos reasons as follows: "If social organization is joined to mythology, one reflecting the other, we are led to consider that there is a common agent in both aspects of the culture. This agent is not the regimentation of marriage, because we are dealing here with a practical, utilitarian, social activity that does not exist in myths, or only exists in an incomplete and disguised manner. This common agent has a psychological aspect. And it appears to be bound to the basic principle of psychological dualism which exists in the individual person or is revealed through the expressions of collective behavior. This is the lesson which myths and the veneration of twins which exist among various peoples around the world teaches us" (61:58).

FETISHISM, TOTEMISM, AND TABOOISM

Other systems of magic have been discovered in addition to magic proper, animism, and religion. For example, there are fetishism, totemism, and tabooism. Based on Freud's criterion I believe that fetishism is produced when the holder of omnipotent ideas turns over a part of this omnipotence to inanimate objects which he can touch. It may even be found in words themselves. The magic of the Bantu sorcerers, the sorcery of the Yorubans, the witchcraft of the Males, talismans and amulets are all fetishes of various types. The magic formulas we already mentioned when discussing oral libido would also fall in this category. (60:208).

Fetishism is also a word used to characterize a certain kind of sexual aberration. As such it becomes a word meaning the inappropriate substitution of the sexual object. In it the normal sexual object is substituted for by another related to it, but at the same time totally inappropriate to serve a normal sexual objective. According to Freud, this substitute for the normal sexual object is in general a part of the body-highly inappropriate for normal sexual purposes (the feet or the hair), or an inanimate object visibly related to the sexual person and especially its sexuality (such as tokens of clothing, underwear, etc.). This substitute is compared, not without reason, to the fetish in which the savage embodies his god (33).

On the other hand, totemism exists when a certain omnipotence of ideas is recognized in plants and animals. Without a doubt this deals with a much more complex system. Consequently magic, animism, religion, fetishism, and totemism are all systems of psychic projection. Spirits, gods, fetishes, totems are all magical symbols of these systems.

To perform perfectly, all these systems require a sequence of prohibitions and restrictions, among which the so-called taboos stand out because of their constraint. I would say that taboos are restrictions with a magical foundation. Prohibitions that have only a moral basis do not fall in this category. The penalty for the transgression of a taboo is always death.

According to Freud, the taboo probably originated from exogamy, since the exogamous institution by itself would have been insufficient to be respected. Incestuous desires would prevail over social formalities. Consequently, these prohibitions were created. Exogamy then is a taboo par excellence. Nevertheless, the taboo transcends the limited scope of exogamy and probably became established as a preventative over everything which could be desired and whose possession contravened the social norms of a people. Freud stated that we cannot in fact see that there would be any need to prohibit what no one wants to do. Only those things which are the objects of a desire are sternly prohibited (34).

In addition we must remember the capacity for transferring a taboo from one object to a substitute object in folklore. This was what Freud implicitly suggested on comparing totemic taboos with the obsessional taboos of the psychopath. One of his patients, for example, required him to remove an object her husband had just brought from the house. She had heard that it had been bought on Ciervos Street. It happened that the name of one of her enemies was Mrs. Ciervos. On the basis of this Freud avers that obsessive prohibitions are capable of extensive transfer. All kinds of plots are used to extend them from one object to another and to make them each impossible. Thus, many times, the entire world ends by being impossible (34).

I have observed that the same thing happens in folklore. The transfer mechanism may be the same, notwithstanding the fact that many prohibitions also become "unexplainable" or appear "stupid and absurd" (34). These systems, as well as the symbols can blend with each other providing variants, syncretic results, typical examples of cultures which transculturate among each other. Thus there can be fetishistic animism, totemic religion, fetishistic religion, etc. And of course there are fetishistic ghosts, totemic gods, fetishistic gods, etc.

The so-called talisman-words or verbal formulas, or even oral fetishes are folkloric examples of fetishism. There is a certain relation between them and man, and Levy-Bruhl's law of participation functions here. Furthermore, they are held to possess a certain amount of the omnipotence of ideas. Thus, by themselves, they have the power to cause good fortune or misfortune. Man considers them valid by themselves—capable of opening caves (Open, Sesame!) and of curing sickness—and these emanate from his psychic projections. The following benediction is common in Morro das Pedras, Minas Gerais, Brazil (it helps to dry the mother's milk so that the ganglions under the arms disappear):

(73) My little maiden star,
      The ganglion said,
      Die that it may live!
      But I say:
      You live, that it may die! (61)

The next benediction, also found there, is for the same purpose. The individual must perform it at a door which has three boards. He must knock his elbow three times on each board for three days saying:

(74) This door has three boards,
      One, two, three,
      But not ganglions at all! (61)

Magical formulas and prayers of evidently fetishistic Catholic syncretism are not rare. For example, when a child is considered beautiful, and to avoid *quebranto* (a kind of evil eye), it is expedient to say at that moment:

(75) May God bless you! (61)

To help a difficult childbirth there is the *Oração de 15 minutos* (the fifteen minute prayer) which is prayed by the midwife with her arms outstretched in the form of a cross next to the parturient bed:

> (76) Oh Blessed Catherine, worthy and beloved, you are the lady who arrived at Abraham's home and found ten thousand men bound up there. You calmed them all with words of reason. So, great saint, calm my heart [or help this birth] so that my heart will be like that of Jesus surrounded by his torturers (61).

Freud was correct in stating that children, like savages, are prisoners of their omnipotence of ideas. They deal with words like objects and they play with words (63). Magic words make magic carpets fly in folkloric fables. Magic words carry the insane from one place to another with the greatest ease. This is the case, for example, of a certain patient of Ramos for whom it was sufficient to invoke a mysterious "power of the ball" to obtain, in Bahia, objects from Rio de Janeiro or from wherever else he fancied (59:323).

For psychiatric purposes, Tanzi labeled this worship of the word on the part of the insane as logolatry. Ramos applied the term in general to the phenomenon—whether among the insane, the savage, or the plebeian. He claimed that logolators were usually those savages who used magical formulas to cure their illnesses (63:175).

While discussing the previously mentioned theory of the transfer of taboos, we noted that, astonishingly, many apparently unexplainable taboos of Paraguayan and other folklores are understandable and even justifiable. The transfer here is from an object which is truly taboo in the unconscious, to a substitute for it—a symbol. The folkloric formula views this symbol as a taboo object; consequently no one knows its cause. The prohibition works out incoherently, inexplicably, confused. Yet once the thing which the symbol stands for is known, the phenomenon becomes understandable. I found many objects—hats, stones, handkerchiefs, arms, coffins, clothes, doves—in my Paraguayan research which were apparently taboo without any reason. When I discovered their unconscious correspondences, it was as if everything had suddenly been made clear. Examples:

> (77) To place hats on the bed is bad luck.

Are not hats symbols of male genitals? (29).

> (78) A pregnant woman must not kill a snake. The infant will crawl in its mother's belly.

Is not the snake also the most important symbol of the male organ? (29). Is there anyone who does not now see that these taboos are for the prohibition of coitus on specified occasions?

Like these, many other examples of taboos ("the avoidances" of the English) appear in Paraguayan folklore:

> (79) Using a mortar at night attracts the hobgoblin.
> (80) Using a mortar when a child is expected causes the child to be overdue or stillborn.
> (81) Using a mortar during Holy Week, after Holy Wednesday, offends God.
> (82) The person who uses a mortar and steps on its rim is always addicted to gossip.

Is it not possible that the mortar is the female sexual symbol? Caskets, boxes, cases, and chimneys equate with the female body as do caves, vessels, and all kinds of containers (29). In turn, the symbolism of the act of using the mortar—that is to say, of ramming it down, of its rhythmic coming and going in a positive and repetitive way—is clearly analogous with coitus.

The manifested content in these items which are taboo corresponds to the following latent contents. In item (79) the sexual act is prohibited at night because this may attract the Evil Father. Specifically, in the Paraguayan region where this very taboo is popular, it is not improbable for the father-in-law to appear at night to recover his daughter, kidnapped by an offending son-in-law. There are even today countless cases of kidnapping and seduction in the Paraguayan family. Since nighttime is the time for love, it is possible that his (the father-in-law's) incursions surprise the lovers during the sexual act. Thus it is that "the mortar should not be used at night, because it attracts the hobgoblin." Item (80) deals with a medical prohibition in that a pregnant woman must abstain. Item (81) is a prohibition with a religious foundation the meaning of which is self-evident. In item (82) we become familiar with the relationship between those who are sexually unsatisfied (interrupted coitus, between the legs, etc.). Their social conduct is characterized by gossip, spite, and oral sadism.

What other explanations can be found for these folkloric acts which are apparently so enigmatic? My theory of taboo symbols stands as a modest contribution to this topic and it will be discussed and developed on another occasion.

In summary, taboos are prohibitions with magical foundations—not merely moral ones. They began from exogamy toward various objects. In this case, things are either directly or indirectly tabooed by the transfer of the taboo. This transfer can, at times, obscure the taboo—especially when it functions with two or more symbols.

As Freud did to dreams, I feel here that symbolic taboos contain two components: the manifest content (which is its folkloric form) and the latent content (which is hidden by the symbol). Furthermore, I feel that the elaboration of the taboo is the process of converting the latent content into the manifest one (a process realized by the populace). Analysis is a contrary process which is realized by the folklorist. He accomplishes the task of observing and analyzing a taboo in the following order:

1. By determining if it is a direct or an indirect taboo.
2. If it is an indirect taboo, by determining if it utilizes a single symbol.
3. By reading about the symbol.
4. By reading about the secondary or tertiary symbols, if they exist, and by determining how each of them is tied in with the preceding one.

Consistent with this classification there is not the least doubt that censure plays a major role in the elaboration of the taboo. The symbolic taboo is unconsciously repressed matter. The formula for such taboos is the same as Freud's for certain classes of dreams, since these are but disguised realizations of repressed desires (29).

We are all the more convinced of this possibility since the recollection of the act which is a violation of taboo elicits nothing but anxiety. The violation of a taboo does not develop pleasant sensations, but rather anxiety—the same as revealing repressed matters in psychoanalysis. Since this is so, the analysis of symbolic taboos can put us on the trail of the complexes of the society being studied.

8

The Oedipus Complex
and Identification

The reader must realize that in the preceding chapter, I did no more than sketch out a few brief ideas on totemism. In fact I proceeded this way simply because, according to the criterion of predominance, it belongs more to the classification of Oedipus complexes than to narcissism. It is incumbent then to consider it in detail here. It will be noted how it appears again in various folkloric types such as feasts, worships, myths, fables, and beliefs.

THE CONCEPT OF TOTEMISM

According to a missionary at the beginning of the eighteenth century, the word totem is etymologically derived from a word belonging to the North American Chippewa tribe. The word means sign or symbol. It was recorded there in several ways: *t'otem, t'otam, do-dam, do-dem, do-daim*, etc. (60:350; 48:63; 23:7). According to Frazer, a totem is a material object which the savage venerates superstitiously because he believes that there exists a special relationship between his own person and each object of this kind (34; 23:7).

Frazer's classical distinction between totem and fetish is contained in this concept. The totem is never a single individual object like a fetish. It is a class or a series of objects which are almost always either plants or animals—objects that are part of a species (23:8; 60:350; 34). The fact that there is a very special relationship between the individual and the totem logically places a certain amount of mutual obligation on both of them. These obligations are conditioned by various kinds of totems.

There are at least three of these varieties or species of totems for man: (1) The tribe's totem (clan-totem), which is common to an entire tribe and which passes from one generation to the next by heredity. (2) The sexual totem (sex-totem), which is common to all men or to all women of a tribe. (3) The individual totem (individual-totem), which is the property of a single individual and can not be passed on to the heirs (23).

The clan totem is unquestionably the most important according to Frazer. Since this is of primary interest in our study of psychoanalytical folklore, I will expand on it. We are dealing with a totem that is religious and social at the same time. As a religious system, it is characterized by a belief that all men must be descended from it. It is a belief which leads them to develop their totemic taboos and to realize acts of identification.

Among these taboos appear those which prohibit killing and eating the totem. At times touching it, even looking at it or saying its name is also prohibited. Frazer cites several examples concerning this:

(83) Among the tribes along the Carpathian Gulf, the man who kills the animal totem is admonished with this question: Why do you want to kill this individual? Do you not, perchance, know that he is my father? (23:20; 60:351).

(84) The Osage Indians never hunt their totem because they might kill a brother (23:20).

Evidently the violation of these prohibitions will bring about various kinds of misfortunes. Identification, in turn, is complete and is characterized by the adoption of physical and moral totemic features. In this way the individual seizes the name of the totem, imitates it outwardly, and is brought to the totemic food, contradicting the taboo, so as to gain the taboo's own power and virtue by ingesting it. The need for identification then conquers the taboo and alternates with it.

(85) The Iroquois consequently call themselves "wolf," "bear," "turtle," and so on. The Bororos are "deer," and "red macaws"; the Guaycurus are "falcons"; the Mibachs of Africa are "spiders," and the Basutos are "crocodiles." The primitive Syrians' totem was

the fish (and because of this, was used to represent Christ at the time they lived in the catacombs). The ancient Romans' was the wolf which was later transformed into the coat of arms of the people (23:13; 48:63).

The imitation of the exterior features is achieved by decoration with skins, tatooing, hair style, and even the extraction of teeth:

(86) The indigenous people of Peru deck themselves out with condor feathers, the creature from which they believe they are descended.

(87) The North American Indians mold a painting or etching of their totemic animal on their skin.

(88) The hairdo of the Little Omahas has the shape of a beak, or a bird's tail, or falls over the ears in the shape of a wing.

(89) The Batokas of Africa pull out their upper incisor teeth to look like an ox. At times they keep them so as to resemble a zebra.

(90) The Manganyas file all their teeth to look like a crocodile or a cat (23).

Such identification takes place primarily during cycles or events dealing with transition (birth, adolescence, marriage, death). Ritualistic dances and pantomimes are then performed.

(91) In Australia a pantomime is performed in which men run about on all fours and howl so as to imitate the dog called *dingo*. The director of the ceremony appears and during a very high leap, claps his hands and says the totemic name "Savage Dog," and the feast ends (23).

Of all aspects of totemic identification, totemic food is without a doubt the most complex since it occurs in spite of the taboo that "Thou shalt not kill!" To relieve the guilt, it is always a collective crime. The feast which follows it, which is mixed with mourning, comes from the feeling of happiness from acquiring the beneficial effects of the totemic sacrifice. At first glance this ritualistic homicide can not be understood and perhaps its demonstrations of festive happiness have been erroneously interpreted as sadism.

Here is a reconstruction of a totemic meal, according to Freud's interpretation:

(92) On a solemn occasion, the clan cruelly kills its totemic animal and eats it raw—blood, meat, and bones. The members of

the clan dress for this ceremony so as to appear like the totem, whose sounds and movements they imitate—as if they wished to project their identity into his. They know that they are carrying out an act which is prohibited for each individual, but which is free from sin from the moment that everyone takes part in it. Furthermore, no one has the right to contrive to avoid it. Once the bloody act has been carried out, the dead animal is grieved for and mourned. The mourning which this death promotes is dictated and imposed through fear of punishment and, according to Robertson Smith when making reference to a similar occasion, has as an objective, above all, of relieving the clan from the responsibility incurred. But this mourning is followed by a merry feast in which unrestrained freedom is given to all the instincts and all kinds of pleasures are permitted. We can without difficulty catch a glimpse here of the nature and the very essence of the feast. A feast is an excess which is not only permitted but commanded—a solemn violation of a prohibition. But the excesses do not depend on the happy state of mind of the men, which results from a specific prescription, but rather it rests on the very nature of the feast, and happiness is produced by the freedom to do what is in normal times vigorously prohibited (34).

Until now we have only mentioned man's obligations to his totem. We have not yet mentioned their opposites, those which the tribe expects of the totem. Let us remember Frazer's opinion that a man is joined to his totem by reciprocal obligations of help and protection. On dedicating his entire worship to it, he requires in return its most effective assistance. In a word, he requires its help to the extent of the favors he bestows on it (23). Examples are as follows:

(93) Among the Moxos of Peru, whose totem is the jaguar, to be eligible for the title of medicine man and to practice this charitable profession, a man must engage in fierce combat with a tiger.

(94) An African tribe of serpent men called *Psylles* ascertains the legitimacy of children by exposing them to snakebites, and those children who are bastards always perish.

Frazer states that there are clans which drive out the individual who was attacked by the totem in the belief that the latter had disowned him. For example:

(95) A Botswanian bitten by a crocodile or wet by water splashed on him by its tail is immediately exiled from the tribe (23).

Legal trials by ordeal originated from this. The totem was given the right to judge such delicate questions as descent or authenticity (23). Other protections of the totem include freeing man from disease and providing him with auguries and warnings:

(96) The presence of a kangaroo totem always announces an impending danger for the coastal dwellers of Murring in New South Wales.

I will not mention any additional ideas on the clan totem as a religious system. As stated before, it is both religious and social. Let us look at it now as a social system. The clan totem is a social system because of its brotherhood and exogamy: by its brotherhood because all the members of its totemic clan consider themselves related to each other and therefore they owe each other mutual help and protection; by its exogamy because sexual relations and marriage with individuals from the same totem is strictly prohibited. Remember that exogamy or the incest taboo can only be understood in relation to the totem (34).

When we outline what we have stated we have:

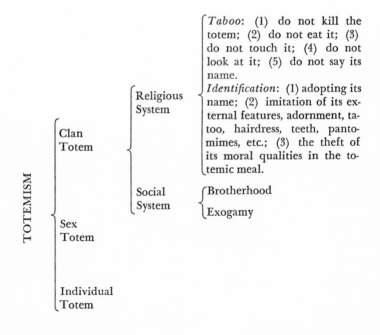

In this framework are included those differentiations made by Frazer which were formulated along general lines, by which the clan totem as a religious system includes man's relations with the totem, and as a social system includes totemic man's relations with totemic man, whether he be from the same or a different totem. It is manifested as a religious system by mutual protection and respect between man and his totem. As a social system it is characterized by certain special relationships between the members of a clan and between the members of different classes (23). Freud believes that from the religious point of view it consists in relationships of respect and mutual regard between man and his totem. From the social point of view it consists in the obligations of the members of the clan to each other and to other tribes (34).

PSYCHOANALYSIS OF TOTEMISM

Now that we have briefly surveyed these essential aspects of totemism from Frazer's important studies we must look at it from the psychoanalytical point of view. Freud placed totemism within the Oedipus complex in *Totem and Taboo*. He began by reviewing the anthropological bibliography of that time: Wundt, *Elementos de la psicología de los pueblos* (1912); S. Reinach, *Cultes, mythes et religions* (1909); Frazer, *Totemism and Exogamy* (1887); A. Lang, *Social Origins* (1903); A. Lang, *Secret of the Totem* (1905); MacLennan, *Primitive Marriage* (1865); Max-Müller, *Contributions to the Science of Mythology* (1897) and Herbert Spencer, *The Origin of Animal Worship* (1870); E. Durkheim, *Les formes elementaires de la vie religieuse. Le système totémique en Australie* (1912); Baldwin Spencer and H. J. Gillen, *The Native Tribes of Central Australia* (1891).

Equipped with this knowledge, he advanced his premise that the totem is the father. To support it he referred to the problem of zoophobia. According to Freud, zoophobia is a psychoneurotic affection characterized by a displacement which ranges from terror of the father to terror of the animal which in some way maintains a relationship with the father. Consequently it is necessarily a displacement which functions when the individual is principally under the influence of the Oedipus complex. Freud states that in such a condition the child finds himself in a mistaken affective arrangement, ambivalent with respect to his father. He mitigates the conflict resulting from this attitude by displacing his hostile and dreadful feelings on a surrogate of the paternal person.

Nevertheless, Freud points out this displacement does not successfully resolve the situation by establishing a definite separation between affectionate and hostile feelings. On the contrary, the conflict and ambivalence persist but they are now directed to the object of the displacement.

It is precisely during this ambivalence, the moment in which fear disappears for a few minutes, that identification develops. The individual identifies himself with the feared animal and plays at running or jumping like him, be it dog or horse, or other animal. The zoophobes, according to Freud, are explained by the Oedipus complex. The father is the animal hated by the child.

Given this first step, Freud was able to advance the idea that fear of the totem is similar to zoophobia, in a general sense from which he concludes by extension that the totem is also the father.

His observations are based primarily on Ferenczi's clinical record of the little Arpad boy. According to Freud the little Arpad boy can be considered as a manifestation of positive totemism in a child (34). Arpad had displaced the feelings which his father aroused by directing them to roosters and hens. His ambivalent attitude toward roosters and hens was evident. He hated them but identified with them on other occasions, changing at that time his human language for the crowing and cackling of the barnyard.

Freud consequently concluded that if totemism finds a correspondent in zoophobia, logic dictates that it must involve processes peculiar to the latter. Totemism recapitulates zoophobia. It is a displacement (transfer) phenomenon which functions precisely in the childhood of the Oedipus complex. Its ambivalence is clear. The two crimes of the Oedipus complex, the death of the father and possession of the mother are well represented there by the violation of the taboos: "Thou shalt not kill the totem" (that is, the father); "Thou shalt not marry someone from your same totem" (exogamy). He stated that if the totemic animal is the father, it follows then that the two principal commandments of totemism, that is, the two principal taboo prescriptions that make up its core—the prohibition of the killing of the totem and that of performing coitus with a woman belonging to the same totem—equate in content with the two crimes of Oedipus who killed his father and married his mother (34).

This series of ideas contributes to the clarification of the previously mentioned mourning and noisy happiness which follow paternal sacrifices. This happiness is produced by the freedom to do what is rigorously prohibited in normal times, while mourning is dictated and imposed by the fear of punishment (34).

Once the father is dead, the individual feels his hatred and his desire for identification suppressed and satisfied. He must permit the return of affectionate feelings for his father. And these feelings in fact do return, but since the father has already been sacrificed they acquire this additional aspect: remorse. They then are feelings of guilt.

With the consciousness of his guilt the individual gives up his former incestuous desires; that is, he renounces gathering up the fruits of his crime. (This is the usual process in daily psychoanalysis.) He renounces them because the dead father has acquired much greater power than he had in life. What the father had formerly prevented by the very fact of his existence, the sons immediately denied themselves as a result of that retrospective obedience which is characteristic of a psychic situation which psychoanalysis has made familiar to us (34).

Under these circumstances the exogamous taboo is present and with greater stability. "Thou shalt not possess thy mother," however, is in part a consequence of the son's guilty conscience who violated it once, performed the paternal sacrifice to repent, and later punished himself. Freud deduced that this is the way that society functions then on the common responsibility of the collective crime, religion on a guilty conscience, and remorse and morals on the needs of a new society and on the expiation required by a guilty conscience. The detailed explanations of these deductions have been omitted, however, from the scope of our work on psychoanalytical folklore. To outline what has been discussed I have organized the following practical correlational table:

Oedipus Complex	Totemism
(Psychoanalysis)	(Anthropology)
1. Desire for the mother.	1. Endogamous taboo.
2. Love and hatred for the father.	2. Totemic taboo.
3. The elimination of the father.	3. Violation of the totemic taboo. The totemic sacrifice.
4. Phallus identification.	4. The totemic meal.
5. Possession of the mother.	5. Violation of the endogamous taboo.
6. Enjoyment resulting from father's death, from identification with him, and from possession of the mother.	6. The totemic feast of sacrifice.
7. Fear of punishment.	7. Totemic mourning.
8. Feelings of guilt, remorse, and self-punishment.	8. *Idem.*
9. Rejection of the fruits of the crime.	9. Purification ceremonies.

The folklorist interested in applying psychoanalysis to totemic folkloric acts will have to first verify the totemic character of these acts and then follow my correlational table. I must point out, however, that collecting, verifying the totemic character, and psychoanalyzing the totemic piece are successive phases and at times these are delayed for generations. This occurred in Brazil. Ramos psychoanalyzed the pieces which his teacher, Nina-Rodrigues, had identified as being totemic. These in turn had been collected by writers during the generations which preceded him.

As previously noted in its ambivalent form, the totem either punishes or rewards the son. When it punishes, this corresponds to the psychological representation of the "dreadful father" which we all possess primarily by virtue of the threat of castration. Since we know there is a counterpart of the Oedipus complex—the Electra complex—it is permissible then to formulate the concept also of a "terrible mother."

We must keep in mind, however, that the evil father as well as the evil mother do not need exclusively totemic acts to appear. When they are not totems in folklore they are phantasmagorical forms, monsters, witches, avenging mother, mothers-in-law (57).

In completing the Freudian outline Rank established that since the totem is the father, the son is the hero or father's assassin. We are dealing with the hero of the general theory of myths, legends, and fables and of Oedipus the incestuous son in psychoanalysis.

Ramos was then led to assimilate these new dimensions and to expound them as well whenever he was faced with certified heroic-mythical characters in Brazilian folklore. He wrote, "The hero is the one who appears in myths as the killer of the father, an authentic totemic monster, and at the same time he is capable of being his substitute. The hero has been converted in the mythical imagination into the ideal of the ego in the same way that the father was the youth's first ideal. The hero comes on stage to accomplish many adventures so as to be able to substitute for the father. With this idealizing of the hero a divinization of the hero is fostered. And since the dead father was not deified it is the hero-god who will announce the primitive father's return (*Urvater*) as a divinity. We then have the following order in the sequence of these divinities: Goddess-mother, hero, God-father. The primitive father is transformed into a divinity then, through the intervention of the son who in this way paid the tribute for the community's offense."

  And he continues, "According to Rank, the hero's birth from a box in the water (the maternal uterus) expresses a reaction to the trauma of birth. . . . But he will unconsciously repeat for the rest of his life, the tendency to return to uterine life—dangerous adventures, until death, and its descent into the bowels of the earth. . . . His rebirth is always covered by a veil of mystery; the hero appears as from the clouds or protected by a rawhide. According to Rank all this indicates a prolongation of the time spent in the uterus. The hero is a reformer and revolutionary in a double sense: in reaction to the primitive libido and in rebellion against the father. His love life is an interminable series of incidents involving the saving of his mother from tyrannical dragons and bad animals. He is the Don Juan of legends and literatures in the conquest of immortality. All the warrior-saints were originally heroes" (60:343–345).

According to Ramos, the hero even develops during the phase of fratricidal struggles, that is, in the matriarchal system, which corresponds to the period of goddess-mothers in the religious realm. Since the mother is a source of anxiety, the masculine gods in this phase are consequently demons. They are phallic entities which become gods only later, with the advent of paternal religion, because paternal religion inspires a group's sublimated anxiety represented by the feeling of guilt.

EXAMPLES

At this point we will consider the folkloric examples of the Oedipus complex. We will make reference to totemism only as needed, since totemism is not the sole class of examples falling in this category. I again use Ramos' material, but in most of the cases I use my own classification criteria.

Totems

One of the best known totemic plays in America is the one about the bull: *Boi-Bumba* in Brazil; *Toro Candil* in Paraguay; *Vaca Loca* in Ecuador; *Toro 'e Candela* in Venezuela. According to Ramos, it is a form of totemism of Bantu origin although it is heavily interspersed with native and Luso-Hispanic elements* (60:361).

In Brazil the characters and dramatic plot vary from area to area although all in all there is a characteristic thematic sequence. This is: (1) A group of characters dance preparing for the stage entrance of the bull; (2) the bull enters on stage led by two or three characters; (3) the bull, tired of dancing, dies; (4) extensive wailing; (5) the doctor comes to cure him; (6) they begin to announce the meal of the bull, during which all its parts are distributed among the spectators; (7) he resurrects to the accompaniment of general applause, either as a result of the medical treatment or because of the effect of the singing while he was divided for the meal.

And the play ends this way. The satisfied group of dancers leave counting the money they received in the house where they were invited to put on the play.

(97) 1. Preparation for the Bull's entrance on stage. *Cavalo-Marinho*

---

*The bull is a wooden carcass covered with an ordinary print material colored red. It represents the body of the animal and its head and horns. This framework is carried about by an individual concealed inside of it (57:106).

[River-horse] and *Arlequim* [Harlequin] dance. The singers sing as follows:

Cavalo-marinho	River-horse,
Vem se apresentar,	Come and introduce yourself
A pedir licença	And ask permission
Para o boi dançar.	For the bull to dance.
Senhô dono da casa,	Mister householder,
Varra o seu terreiro,	Sweep your terreiro,*
Para o boi dançar	So the bull can dance
Mais o seu vaqueiro.	With his cowboy.
Cavalo-marinho	River-horse,
Por tua tenção	In your kindness,
Faz uma mesura	Come, pay compliments
A seu capitão.	To your leader.
Cavalo-marinho,	River-horse,
Dos laços de fitas,	Of ribbon bows,
Faz uma mesura	Pay compliments
Às moças bonitas.	To the pretty girls.
Cavalo-marinho	River-horse,
Chega pra diente,	Come forward.
Faz uma mesura	Pay compliments
A esta toda gente.	To all these people.
Cavalo-marinho	River-horse,
Dança muito bem,	You dance very well,
Pode-se chamar	You could call yourself
Maricas meu bem.	A queer, my dear.
Cavalo-marinho	River-horse,
Dança bem bahiano,	Dances very "Bahian,"
Ben parece ser	Appearing to even be
Um pernambucano.	A Pernambucan.
Cavalo-marinho	River-horse,
Vai para a escola	Go to school
Aprender a ler	To learn to read
E a tocar viola.	And to play the cittern.
Cavalo-marinho	River-horse,
Sabe conviver,	You know how to live with others
Dança o teu bahiano	Dance your "Bahian" dance.
Que eu quero ver.	'Cause I'd like to see it.

*Place where fetishism is practiced.

Cavalo-marinho,	A river-horse,
Eu tomara já,	I'd like to be
Faça uma voltinha	Take a little turn
Vá pra seu lugar.	And go to your place.
Cavalo-marinho	River-horse,
Dança no terreiro,	Dance around the terreiro,
Que o dono da casa	'Cause the householder
Tem muito dinheiro.	Has lots of money.
Cavalo-marinho	River-horse,
Dança na calçada,	Dance on the sidewalk,
Que o dono da casa	'Cause the householder
Tem galinha assada.	Has some roast chicken.
Cavalo-marinho	River-horse,
Dança no tijolo,	Dance on the brick,
Que o dono da casa	'Cause the householder
Tem cordão de ouro.	Has a gold chain.
Cavalo-marinho	River-horse,
Você já dançou,	You've already danced.
Mas porém lá vai,	Nevertheless please accept
Tome lá que eu dou.	What I give you.
Cavalo-marinho	River-horse,
Vamo-nos embora,	Let's go now.
Faz uma mesura	Pay compliments
À tua senhora.	To your wife.
Cavalo-marinho	River-horse,
Vamo-nos embora,	Let's go now.
Já deu meia-noite,	It's past midnight,
Já deu nove horas.	It's already nine o'clock.
Cavalo-marinho,	River-horse,
Por tua mercê,	Through your grace,
Manda vir o boi	Order the Bull to come
Para o povo ver.	So the people can see him.

2. The Bull comes on stage:

River-horse and Harlequin have a dialogue in verse concerning the Bull who does not appear. They ask Matthew, another character who is supposed to carry the Bull, about it. When the Bull appears the singers break out in chorus:

> Come my ornate bull,
> Come and be fierce,
> Come and dance prettily,
> Come and pay compliments,
> Come and do tricks,
> Come and be handsome,
> Come and show what you know naturally.

> Come and dance my bull,
> Play around the grounds,
> Because the householder
> Has lots of money.
> This pretty bull
> Must not die,
> 'Cause he was only born
> To live together with others (9).

Then the Bull begins his wild pranks* following Matthew's orders and attacking the spectators and the characters in the midst of a great hubbub as follows:

MATTHEW: Oh Bull! Hit them with your flanks.
SINGERS: Ei-bumba.
MATTHEW: Knock these people over.
SINGERS: Ei-bumba.
MATTHEW: Hit them with your rump.
SINGERS: Ei-bumba.
MATTHEW: Hit them head-on.
SINGERS: Ei-bumba.
MATTHEW: Come lower down.
SINGERS: Ei-bumba.
MATTHEW: And graze along the terreiro.
SINGERS: Ei-bumba.
MATTHEW: And hit Father Fidere (Fidelis).
SINGERS: Ei-bumba.
MATTHEW: Scare Bastian ...
SINGERS: Ei-bumba.
MATTHEW: Come alongside of me.
SINGERS: Ei-bumba.
MATTHEW: Nice and slow.
SINGERS: Ei-bumba.
MATTHEW: Go ahead and strike out in front.
SINGERS: Ei-bumba.
MATTHEW: Hit the River-horse.
SINGERS: Ei-bumba.
MATTHEW: Oh, Oh, bull of mine.
SINGERS: Ei-bumba.

*In Asunción, Paraguay we attended the performance of this same scene, without verses. It was the "Toro Candil," who frightened the spectators with his horns on fire. We wrote then, "The public participates in the play forming a ring around the bull and the bullfighters. They point out and suggest that he attack a given person. They push others into the path of the one who is attacked. And above all they shout and laugh. The children take an active part in all of it. The young ladies almost always make up the first line. They are the object of real or simulated attacks, as much from the bull as from the bullfighters. And in the melee there is an inordinate mixture of shoving and trampling" (17).

MATTHEW: Come out of that house.
  SINGERS: Ei-bumba.
MATTHEW: Dance prettily now.
  SINGERS: Ei-bumba.
MATTHEW: In the middle of the square.
  SINGERS: Ei-bumba.
MATTHEW: Play the cittern.
  SINGERS: Ei-bumba.
MATTHEW: Smite them well.
  SINGERS: Ei-bumba.
MATTHEW: Dance lots and lots.

3. The death of the Bull.
In the middle of a given song Matthew shouts out in despair:

Stop, stop, stop!
I have news for you!
The Bull danced and danced
But now he is lying down.

They realize that the Bull is dead. They blame Matthew. The Captain angrily punishes him and forces him to go call the Doctor in a hurry.

4. Wailing, mourning.
SEBASTIAN: Ay friend of mine!
           The Master's Bull died ...
SEBASTIAN: My Bull died!
           What will happen to me?
           Send for another
           Over there in Piauí.*
CAPTAIN: Oh Matthew, where's the bull?
MATTHEW: Sir, the Bull died ... (60:362–368).

5. The Doctor's Treatment.
The Doctor orders a lengthy prescription and concludes by ordering an enema for the Bull. At this the Bull gets up (according to Pereira da Costa's version). In other versions the Doctor shares him among those who are present before the Bull comes to life.

6. The Bull's "Last Will and Testament."
The Bull's hide.
Xaxou!

The tail
Is for my chuma.

And the shin bone
Is for Don Yaco.

*Piauí, a State in Brazil.

A hind hoof and a fore hoof
Is for the Captain, sir.

The skinny belly
Is for my queen.

The parts of the liver
Are for my friend.

And the lungs
Are for a box of matches.

The front of the Bull
Is for Matthew and the clown.

The tip of the horns
Is to make a pipe bowl.

And the spleen
Is for my queen.

The Bull's liver
Is for the two of you.

The kidney
Is not for me.

I already sold the horn.
Xaxou!

And the throat
Is for a single girl.

And the snack
Is for Don Ventania.

The black-pudding filling
Is for Don Anastasius.

The fore-quarter
Is for Don Monteiro.

The quarter on this side
Is for Don Rosalvo.

And the smallest breast
Is for old Manuela.

The short ribs
Are for little Mistress Naninha.

(This is according to Arthur Ramos' version, 57:109–11. See another version in Carneiro, 10:172–174.)

7. The Bull's resurrection, applause, end of the feast.

Ramos should have applied psychoanalysis to it in clear language. He did not do so immediately, however, and limited himself to stating, "We have the totemic-psychoanalytical motives here which we are examining" (60:372). I feel encouraged to do so myself, and have developed the following correlational outline:

Bumba-meu-boi	Psychoanalysis
1. The Bull's death	1. Is the possible elimination of the father.
2. The Bull's "Last Will and Testament" (A totemic meal)	2. Is the supreme moment of identification with the father.
3. Wailing, shameless cries, despair because of the Bull's death	3. Is fear of punishment.
4. The Bull's resurrection	4. Is the solution found in the ego resulting from the cruel pressure of the superego.

Several years later in his *Estudos de folklore*, Ramos wrote, "We have in this popular story the symbolic representation of the primitive tragedy of the father's death and the consecutive components of the children's contrition, the advent of a martyr who is going to expiate their guilt, the return of a deified father." On comparing the *Bumba-meu-boi* with other plays which are totemic survivances, he added: "The totemic complexes in the *Bumba-meu-boi* play appear with greater certainty with the Bull's (Father's) death as the *leitmotiv*. In some versions there is the Bull's last will and testament which recalls the theme of the totemic meal, symbolic communion, an ancient theme in religion. All are redeemed after this communion. The Father returns deified, comes down over the group, and envelops it in a protective embrace" (56:176, 178–179).

In his criticism of Ramos' psychoanalytical interpretation Carneiro expresses his preference for dialectical materialism. He states, however, that perhaps Ramos is right. This means that it is possible that the Bull's last will and testament corresponds in fact to the totemic meal. First of all, however, this phenomenon is no doubt the result of the evolution of the productive forces of society (10:176).

The "Burial of the Bull's Head" is an event in the same cycle of the Bull which we already mentioned. Ramos recalls having witnessed it in Alagoas during the January feasts:

(98) The skeleton of a bull's head with its appropriate horns (or an analogous artificial framework) is placed in a cart pulled by an ox. The cart is all decked out with leaves, palm and tree branches. During the afternoon on the Feast of the Kings it is taken out on the street with a big retinue, rockets going off, music and shouting and at the head of the cortege, an individual who is called Matthew who cries out as he leads the bull:
Eh boi, eh boi ... (Hey bull, hey bull ...)
The cortege goes through all the streets of the town giving out "firewater" to the townspeople from a barrel in the back of the cart. In the city of Pilar (in Alagoas) the burial of the bull's head coincides with the ceremony of the erection of the staff of the town's patron saint.

"What meaning unknown to the masses, does this symbolic ceremony express?" Ramos asks. He then states, "The burial of the bull is nothing more than a totemic survival. It is the father-totem who is dead and buried in the midst of all these demonstrations of joy. Matthew is the hero-son who is going to sacrifice himself for his assassin brothers, and he shifts the responsibility for the crime to himself. The raising of the staff has a phallic significance. It is the inheritance of paternal attributes by rebellious children. And the patron saint whose celebration will began immediately expresses the beginning of the matriarchate and the epoch of goddess-mothers who survived the death of the father (note that the feast of Our Lady of Pilar continues until February second)" (60:373–374).

Ramos states that the *"congos"* or *"cucumbis"* are historical survivals with totemic elements which have been stuck on them a posteriori. Like the bull they present characters which have several variants and a dramatical sequence in accordance with the area in Brazil where it is observed. It is nevertheless possible to identify the basic thematic sequence: (1) The Queen sends her ambassador to the court of King Congo; (2) various problems arise in the midst of which Mamêto appears and asks for the Ambassador's apology; (3) the battle begins and Mamêto dies (in some versions he is killed by an Amerindian individual: a Caboclo with a tragic expression who brandishes a terrible club); (4) But the witch doctor has the power of bringing Mamêto back to life, doing this with sayings, magical passes, and chants which are answered in chorus. Mamêto revives to the accompaniment of great joy and the play ends with dances and chants which celebrate the event" (57:43).

Let us examine this selection in detail:

(99) 1. The Queen sends her ambassador to the court of King Congo. It is the time for the exchange of greetings. The Cucumbis dance and sing, among others, the following verses:

Hey . . . Hey there, weakling,
I've just come from Portugal.
CHORUS: With the permission, *auê* . . .
          With the permission, *auê* . . . !
          With the permission of the head of the house,
          With the permission, *auê* . . . !

2. Mamêto appears.

He performs dances which imitate the wriggling of snakes, the lithe leap of the jaguar, the rocking of the black slave ships on a calm sea.

3. The battle and Mamêto's death.

The Caboclo (half-breed) mortally wounds Mamêto, creating great anxiety. But the Cucumbis with heads bowed begin a wake over the body with uninterrupted funereal wails:

Mala quilombê, ô quilombâ . . .
Oh Mamêto, Oh eh!
Mala quilombê, ô quilombâ . . . *

The Chief of the Congos, perplexed and overwhelmed by the weight of responsibility, designates The Tongue to go to tell the Queen, the mother of Mamêto the Prince, the unfortunate event. The Queen listens to the emissary and then raves in anguish. She orders Quimboto, the witch doctor to bring Mamêto back to life and threatens that she will cut off his head if he is not successful.

4. Mamêto's resurrection.

Looking at the bearers surrounding Mamêto's corpse the witch doctor sings mournfully:

          E . . . Mamaô! E . . . Mamaô!
          Ganga rumbá, sinderê iacô.
          E . . . Mamaô! E . . . Mamaô!
CHORUS: *Zumbi, matêquerê,*
          Congo, cucumbi-óyá.
WITCH DOCTOR: *Zumbi, Zumbi, oia Zumbi!*
          Oia Mamêto muchicongo.
          Oia papêto.
CHORUS: *Zumbi, Zumbi, oia Zumbi!* **

---

*Brazilian deformed survivances of old African languages.

**Brazilian African language. Some words are still clear, like Zumbi, who was a great leader of the black slaves. Brazilian Negro slaves rebelled many times. Like Spartacus during Rome's empire, in Brazil Zumbi escaped and attracted thousands of comrades who for years resisted their masters' attacks in a region called Palmares. His so-called Palmares Republic was organized according to African models.

Mello Moraes says that "During all these evocations the witch doctor circles the child's body, examines it, feels it, makes magical passes, uses mysterious items of sorcery, makes him breathe in plants and resins, and lays out little snakes and talismen with supernatural qualities alongside of him. The Cucumbis and the magician note that little by little the dead one is coming back to life. The Rancho (the group of Cucumbis) feel happy and the witch doctor intones the following as the crowd shakes its instruments:

WITCH DOCTOR: Quimboto, Quimboto,
    Quimboto arara ...
CHORUS: Savatá ó Lengua.
WITCH DOCTOR: Who can do more?
CHORUS: The sun and the moon.
WITCH DOCTOR: The greatest saint?
CHORUS: Is Saint Benedict.

"When the dialogue is finished during which the native men and women dance and sing with incredible originality the witch doctor throws himself at the feet of the prince. He takes him by the hand, raises him slowly, and sings with superstitious ecstasy, as if he were slowly awakening him:

WITCH DOCTOR: Tatarana, *ai auê* ...
    Tatarana, *tuca, tuca,*
    tuca, auê ...

"As soon as Mamêto is revived, with greater agility and warmth and faster than the others, he executes wonderful dance steps. The witch doctor strikes the Caboclo with but a glance and he falls to the ground. As a result of new enchantments, the latter comes back to life. He again attempts to kill the Prince of the Congos and a heated battle between the two tribes begins. The enemies are conquered. After the victory Mamêto is presented to the Queen, who receives him with open arms, and then showers the witch doctor with precious gifts. The King gives him (the witch doctor) his daughter in marriage, but the latter does not accept since he is already married."

5. End of the feast. Unusual happiness of the Cucumbis.

"Marches, countermarches, dances, and songs announce the end of the ballet. They then beat their tambourines, shake their *canzás* (a hollow gourd containing dried seeds), and beat their drums.

CHORUS: *Maria, rabúla auê* ...
    Catumga auê ...
FOREMAN: Good-bye, my love,
    Good-bye, my love.
ALL (leaving the stage): In Bahia there is,
    There is, there is,
    In Bahia there is,
    Oh Bahian gal,
    Water for a penny ..."

(This version by Mello Moraes Filho, 57:44–41; Cf. 50:167–178.)

This is a play containing without question certain historical survivals. According to Ramos, "We can identify the following themes in it: (a) The coronation ceremony of the ancient monarchs of the Congo; (b) battles of these monarchies against each other; (c) battles against invading colonizers; (d) various historical episodes including the exchange of embassies, predictions of witch doctors, etc." (57:56–57).

According to psychoanalysis, the dispute between the King of the Congo and Queen Ginga is a recollection of the matriarchal wars mentioned by African historians. Although the father's death does not appear in the play, the son's return is a fact. The hero-son Mamêto, is sacrificed because he violated the endogamic taboo. But the collective feeling of guilt grows and is assuaged by the son's resurrection (57:63; 56:1–7; 178).

Iemanjá (which is pronounced as "Iemenyá" is a myth, a worship, or a tale in Afro-Brazilian folklore. According to Ramos, it came with the Gêges, Nagós, and Minas, Negroes from the slave coast. It was later amalgamated with the European-Brazilian folklore about sirens, the American folklore about the Mother of the Water, and Catholicism and its Our Lady of the Rosary (60:306).

(100) The ceremony of giving gifts to the Mother of the water is one of the most impressive in Bahia. Every year the Dique, Montserrat, Cabrito, and other places in Bahia receive the large votive procession of those who are going to bring their gift to the mother. The *pai do santo* (father of the saint), the priest in indigenous Negro rites, directs the veneration dressed in white. Iemanjá's white standard is carried at the head of the procession of twenty or thirty persons. The gifts are carried on their heads. They include pitchers of water, beautiful boxes adorned with ribbons and flowers; fans, face powder, soap, combs, and bottles of perfume inside the boxes, Iemanjá needs all of these for her toilette. They sing Iemanjá's songs. Believers in Iemanjá sometimes board small sailboats to throw the gifts far away (60:306–307).

Reports in the newspaper about the event read this way: "They gave her an obvious shape, the flowing body of a woman, pink flesh, and passionately thrust breasts. Her face is beautiful and her head is adorned with long green hair. She lacks lower limbs. In their place she has the long scaly tail of a fish. Hundreds of *saveiros* (a small sailboat) and *jangadas* (a balsa wood sailing raft) filled with both beginners and those initiated in the worship of the Mother of the Water, largely fishermen and their families, meet a precise place at sea, form a circle at the indicated location as the probable residence of their idol with the green hair and hypnotic glances. After a brief silence and at a prearranged signal, the presents for the miraculous vision are thrown into the sea. And the sad melody of a mournful chant is sung by the entire seagoing procession. On returning from the feast of the Mother of the Water each and every one feels he has the right to hope for a miracle" (60:311).

The following is apt to be heard in the syncretic *candomblé* and *macumba* chants:

Along the shores of the river I found
A siren praising the saints,
A princess, queen of the sea,
Princess! A sailor is coming now! (60:308).

Ramos attempts to achieve the psychoanalysis of this worship, evaluating it from three points of view: as a maternal image, as incest, and as punishment. In the first instance Iemanjá is the maternal image, a statement which can be proved by the following observations. (1) The mother idea is constant—they call Iemanjá Mother and Mother of the Water, (2) She is frequently represented in *candomblés* in feminine form, with large breasts symbolizing fertility, even though her fetish is a maritime stone. In the *candomblés de caboclo*, a kind of voodoo rite, she becomes the siren and as such is represented by a figure which is half fish and half woman with beautiful features and long tresses. (3) Other features also accent her maternal attributes. For example, the kinds of gifts they offer her: face soap, bottles of perfume, ribbons, and combs. (4) She protects, helps the afflicted, resolves questions and problems of daily living, and consoles the unfortunate, as is the case in maternal worship in all religions. (5) And she is bound to water which, psychoanalytically speaking, must not be overlooked as being a symbol related to the maternal complex. Dreams about water are dreams about birth (60:305–310).

In support of his view Ramos cites Jung who states that the sea was the genesis symbol for the ancients, and from it came life, Christ, and Mithras also. Mithras is represented as being born on the banks of a river. Every living thing comes from the water, such as the sun, and at nightfall it sets in it again. Born from streams, rivers, or seas man at death comes to the Stygian waters to begin his nocturnal sea journey. These dark waters of death are waters of life. Death with its cold embrace is the mother's breast, the same as the sea, which although it swallows the sun, brings it forth again from its innermost recesses. (44)

In addition Ramos recalls P. Sébillot who in his *Le Folklore* (1913) collected beliefs related to water and concluded that water in the many folklores exercises an influence on fertility, the abundance of milk, etc. (60) The sea is definitely an ancient maternal symbol.

When this premise is understood, the one that Iemanjá is a maternal image, it obviously clarifies the question of the unconscious attraction she has for her believers. Newspapers in their accounts of police matters relate cases of persons attracted by her song who were dragged down into the vortex of her waves. For example, here is the statement of a witch doctor to the police concerning the death of Eusebio, a blind man, that he had brought to the Mother of the Water to be cured: "Eusebio was called by the Mother of the Water. He lost his balance (on a rock) and fell (into the water). It was an act of fate" (60:322). Excerpts from a suicide note: "My darling husband Cezarino. I long for you greatly. I am writing you in Niteroi. It is the last time because I am going to throw myself into the water. I hear a voice all the time which is calling to me to die. I don't know what it is but I am going anyhow. You know I'm from the water don't you? When I was crying I could not tell what I felt but I was hearing the voice" (60:322–323). There are exquisite pages about Iemanjá in Jorge Amado's novels. They are an important lyrical theme about enchantment and damnation.

In conclusion Ramos states, "The attraction of the water, Lorelei's spell with her long golden hair, her intoxicating voice coming from the depths of the water, the siren's chant, the bewitchment of Iara and Iemanjá express nothing else than incestuous attraction, the unconscious desire to return to the maternal breast" (60:317).

Punishment also comes, however, because incest is taboo. "Woe be unto the one who lets himself be duped by the fatal attraction of the Mother of the Water. His body will be dragged down to the vortices of the dark abysses. It is Oedipus' punishment for violating the maternal incest taboo!" (60:317).

These psychoanalytical motives found in the Afro-Brazilian worship of Iemanjá: the maternal image, the incestuous attraction, punishment, also appear in the syncretic tales of Iemanjá, the tales about the Mother of the Water. According to Ramos, "In plebeian Brazilian tales about the Mother of the Water, the punishment motive, although disguised due to the emphasis of the Oedipus complex, appears with astonishing frequency" (60:323). As an example he cites the following version reported by J. da Silva Campos from Bahia:

(101) He was a very poor man and whenever he went to the cliff he met the Mother of the Water seated on a boulder on the river bank with her tresses flowing. One day he went slowly and grabbed her by the shoulder. After a tremendous struggle he succeeded in bringing her home and marrying her. But she warned him before marrying him never to curse the people under the water.

From the time of the man's marriage to the Mother of the Water things went so well for him that it was astounding. He built a very beautiful house several stories high and had many slaves, cattle, and a great deal of land. At the outset he lived in harmony with his wife. But when she felt like going away she began to annoy him every day and by every means and method possible. The house was always disarranged and unswept, the meals were badly prepared, and the children were dirty and did not pay any attention to his words of advice. Even the slaves disobeyed him. There was such disorder in the house that it was almost frightening. All this was only to make him angry. One day the man could stand this inferno no longer and, sick of his humiliation, he said very softly, "Damn those people under the water!"

At that very instant the young woman got up from the chair where she was sitting and he heard a very loud crash—BANG!! A tremendous hole opened up in the floor of the room and she began to sing:

> People of mine,
> What happened is wonderful.
> Let's all go away.

On hearing this voice those who were in the house, children, slaves, and servants, joined the others at the edge of the hole and fell into it. When this great crowd of people had finished falling in she sang:

> All this money, etc. . . .

And the money which was in the house, gold, silver, and copper coins fell into the well: clink, clink! Then she sang:

> All these animals, etc. . . .

Then all the bulls, cows, pigs, lambs, chickens, in fact, everything that was an animal went into the hole. Then she sang:

> All these furnishings, etc. . . .

All the furniture, dishes, chests, and other furnishings went. At the
end she sang:

               Also this house, etc. . . .

The house fell into the hole, and she fell in behind the house. Everything was transformed into earth, and then the hole disappeared.
The man was left poor, poor like he had been before (60:326; cf.
48:249).

It appeared to Ramos that this symbolism of the water, and the
respect for aquatic totemic entities was so great that the custom
of blessing the waters and of blessing one's self on entering the
water were superstitious practices derived from them. (60:330)
In the final analysis the fear of punishment by maritime monsters,
the symbols of the evil mother, explain these practices. Consequently, we can understand the practices for diagnosis and treatment of paralysis found in the folklore of Montevideo. We collected the following from a medicaster:

> (102) The medicaster uses water in a glass. She blesses it in the
> name of the Father, with prayers and crosses on the rim of the glass.
> She conjoins the patient's name to a piece of coal which she throws
> into the water. If the coal goes to the bottom, it is because the
> patient is sick (16).

From a psychoanalytical viewpoint the water may symbolize the
maternal image and the coal the son. The medicaster unconsciously identifies the latter as the client as a result of the omnipotence of her ideas. The paralytic symptoms represent the fear
of punishment. The magical practice in its entirety is a reproduction of an incestuous scene. The coal (the son) is attracted by the
water (the mother). If the coal goes to the bottom of the water it
is because the incest was consummated, that is, the client trans-
gressed the taboo (of not exposing his sweaty shoulders to the
wind). The prayers, blessings, and benedictions of the medicaster
are samples of the feelings of guilt. She and her client punish themselves this way three times a day for three consecutive days, at the
end of which the son (the client) leaves relieved (cured).

This analysis becomes more probable if we consider the fact that
the coal must be lighted, and because of this it is thrown into the
water with a spoon. The lighted coal is a pleonasm, since in psychoanalysis the symbolism for fire includes coal and lighted coal.

As we have seen, fire is the libido. Fire describes Xango the Afro-Brazilian phallic fetishist deity, while water is a feminine abode. Fire in the water, a lighted coal thrown into the water symbolizes the scene of the sexual act (26:134, 140).

The lighted coal portrays the son at the peak of his potency. Three coals are thrown in the water, one on each occasion and accompanied by prayers. This signifies the mother's repeated temptations. The son consents to one of them, or at no time consents to any of them, since he has overcome the incestuous attraction. The son is not "paralyzed" (guilty) if the coal floats three times. Furthermore, according to Freud the number three is a proven symbol for the male genitals (29; 26).

The Kibungo (*quibungo, chibungo, n'bungo, Tchimbungu*) is another Afro-Brazilian totemic entity. Like Iemanjá he is half-human and half-animal. The difference lies in that he lives in the woods and not at sea. He is also called *Lobisomen* (wolf-man) in Brazil. The latter is the syncretic result of variants of European origin (*loup-garou, wolf-gürter*, etc.) with the authentically African variant of the *kibungu*. He is also found in the Rio de la Plata region as the "black-dog" (39).

(103) In the opinion of the Sertanejos (those from deep in the northeast hinterlands), all very pale and anemic men or those suffering from ancylostomiasis are called *amarelos* (yellow men), *empambados* (anemic), and *comem-longe* (geophagist). During the night from Thursday to Friday they change themselves into wolves or large dogs, turning their clothes inside out and rubbing themselves back and forth with horse dung. Then their ears grow like fans, fall on their shoulders, and wave like the wings of a bat. Their faces become hideous, half-wolf or dog, and half-man. Afterwards these unfortunate men go out and run along the roads crazily fulfilling their sad fate (3:569).

This Afro-Brazilian wolf-man is a totemic survival, according to Ramos, and it explains the motive for people believing they transform themselves into werewolves. This transformation process is an unconscious process of identification with the father who in this case is the totem. He is in turn the leopard in Oceania, the hyenna in Africa, the wolf in Germany, France, and Africa (wolf, *loup, kibungo*), the tiger in India, and the black dog in Argentina.

Ramos cites Dias de Carvalho to prove the totemic origin. The latter states that in Africa the *chibungo* is the "protector of his own kind. He leads them away from snares and traps and in turn no hunter dares to point his weapon at them. The *chibungo* does not speak before more important people. He imitates the animal's distrustful looks, his appearance, calls, and nervous manner of attacking. On entering a circle of bystanders, his greeting is announced like all the others by sacramental applause and is limited to a glance to each side and some deep guttural grunts until the sovereign notices him and raises his right hand as a signal of thanks for his greeting. The *chibungo* emits a brief sound accompanied by the lowering of his head to mean the affirmative. The negative is expressed by stretching the sound out and turning the head to the right as if annoyed. The *chibungo* only speaks when questioned by the sovereign. He always attempts to accompany his speech by mimicry as well as giving his face the animal expression which it attempts to represent" (57:198).

Commenting on Gustavo Barroso's version, Ramos adds, "In Brazil those ill with jaundice, the *empabados*, the *comemlonges*, exhausted by anemia, transform themselves into werewolves during the night from Thursday to Friday. There is a basis of truth in this belief. Ancylostomyasis, occasioning cenesthesic outbreaks can occasion cenesthesic symptoms of hallucinations among weak individuals and those so mentally predisposed. It can even lead to phenomena where the personality is transformed" (60:276).

The Evil Father

The following are selections in which the Evil Father predominates:

> (104) "Hairy-hands" is a body with a slender human shape with hands made of hanks of hair. He goes about wrapped up in white robes. Adults use him to threaten children by telling them, for example, "Look, if the little boy pees in his bed, Hairy-hands will come and cut the little boy's pecker off!" (48:113–114).

We have already looked at the tale of the Little Girl with the Gold Earrings and its scatological symbols. According to Ramos the terrible father in it is the ugly old man with the sack who put the little girl with the gold earrings in it and threatened her:

> Sing, sing my sack.
> If not I'll hit you with this club.

The psychoanalysis of this selection can be accomplished as follows. (1) The closed space (the old man's sack) symbolizes the maternal uterus. (2) The regression to the maternal uterus is a violation of the incest taboo. This is to say, the son possesses the mother. (3) Retention in the closed space is paternal punishment. This punishment is very clear in the threats with the cane: "I'll hit you with this club." (4) Emerging from the mother's belly (from inside of the sack), alive or not, is nothing more than an infantile fantasy about childbirth and a reaction to the trauma of birth which is related to the myths about the hero's birth (57:230; 56:165–166).

(105) In the tale about an ugly, fat toad a young fellow was madly in love with a girl. He therefore asked for her hand in marriage. But the girl said that she did not want to marry him. The young fellow became angry and began to look for ways and means of killing her. He bewitched a fat toad and he paid a servant in her house to put it under the bench on which she sat while sewing.

Immediately, the girl began to get thin and to look sallow. One day early in the morning, after she had awakened very early to sew, the toad came out from under her bench and grabbed her. The girl then called out to the people in the house who were still asleep:

> Father, Mother,
> Relatives, brothers, and sisters,
> Come. The fat toad
> wants to eat me.

But they had all been bewitched and did not hear the girl's voice but continued to sleep. The toad swallowed her feet while making the following sounds:

> Indunga ... Indunga ... Indunga
> Indunga, Lacadunga, Inguti ...

The girl again called to her family but they continued to sleep like logs. To make the story short, the toad swallowed her whole, while continuing to make the above sounds. And the girl called to her family constantly. They awoke only after the toad had swallowed her. They then found the animal spread out in the living room with the poor girl in its belly. They did not attempt to find out anything about it. They hit it hard, whack, whack, until they killed it, and recovered the girl, still alive, from its belly (48:212).

The threatening and cannibalistic maternal or paternal image is a toad. Some of the same themes as in The Little Girl with the Gold Earrings appear here too, such as the return to a closed space and the girl's escape from this space while still alive. This represents the violation of the maternal taboo and infantile fantasies about birth.

In Afro-Brazilian tales, according to Ramos, the Kibungo continues being totemic, half-man and half-animal, as are the beliefs about him. But the Oedipus themes are more clearly outlined in the tales. In them Kibungo discharges his role as the Evil Father at the same time as the themes of incest, punishment, infantile fantasies about birth, and the castration and anxiety complexes appear more clearly.

(106) Kibungo is a beast, half-man and half-animal. His head is very large and he also has a large hole in the middle of his shoulder which opens when he lowers his head and closes when he raises it. He eats children by lowering his head, opening the hole, and throwing the children in it.

One day a man who had three sons left his house for work, leaving his three children and his wife alone. Kibungo then appeared. Arriving at the door of the house he asked, singing:

Whose house is this?
Auê,
Como gerê, como gerê,
Como êrá?*

The woman answered, trying to speak in his language:

This house belongs to my husband,
Oh there.
That's whose it can be, that's whose it can be.
That's whose it is!

He asked the same question about the children, and she answered that they were hers. Then he said:

Then I want to eat them,
Auê, etc.

She answered:

You can eat them, but
Auê, etc.

*Supposed to be the proper style of Kibungo's speech.

And he ate the three of them together, throwing them into the hole in his shoulder. He then asked the woman to whom she belonged and she said to her husband. The Kibungo decided to eat her also. When he was going to throw her into the hole her husband arrived with a shotgun which frightened the Kibungo a great deal. In his fright Kibungo ran through the middle of the house to flee by the back door. He did not find one because Negroes' houses have only one door. Then he sang:

> The devil with this house,
> *Auê,* etc.
> Which has only one door,
> *Auê,* etc.
> *Como gerê, como gerê,*
> *Como êrá.*

The man came in, shot the Kibungo, killed him, and recovered his children from the hole in his shoulder. He entered by one door, and left by a penknife. My Lord, the King, count up to seven for me! (53:301–303; 57:199–201).

The Kibungo here is doubtlessly the paternal or maternal image who follows, punishes, and devours. It is an image which has an attraction, the space in its shoulder where people fall in. In this sense this tale belongs to the same psychological series as The Fat Ugly Toad and The Little Girl with the Gold Earrings (56:166).

"Kibungo and his son Johnny" is a tale of terror in which the character even devours his own children like the story of Cronus from classical mythology (57:230).

(107) Once upon a time there was a kibungo who married a Negress and had many children by her. But he ate all his children. The woman hid in a hole the last one that was born so that the kibungo would not eat him. His name was Johnny, and his mother warned him at length that when his father would come back from the woods and call for him in a very deep voice, he should not get out of the hole. When she would call to feed him she would always call him with a woman's soft voice which the child knew so well. Well one day when the kibungo did not find any animals to eat in the woods, nor children to devour in town (where he went at night), he returned home very weak. There was no other meat there than that of his child who was hidden. Then because of his weakness, in a soft voice he sang:

> I'm bringing you a cavy, my son!
> I'm bringing you a cavy, my son!

Thinking it was his mother who was returning from town and bringing him the food he liked so well Johnny got out of his hole

and the kibungo grabbed him to eat him. Crying, poor Johnny
sang:
> My mother always told me
> the kibungo would eat me . . .
> My mother always told me
> the kibungo would eat me . . .

And the kibungo ate the last child, and the mother died with grief.
And it is for this reason that the kibungo no longer has a wife or
children (48:111–112; 57:202).

Feminine entities may appear disguised as masculine ones as in
the tale of The Death of Yara's Son. This preoccupied folklorists
because they could find no explanation for it. Ramos states that
psychoanalysis provides an explanation, and suggests that it is a
merging of the castrating Evil Father with the Evil Mother, the
phallic monster (60:329, 331). Thus several Brazilian legends of
the cycle of the Mother of the Water reveal masculine entities.
Iemanjá is converted into a phallic monster:

> (108) At the beginning of the world, according to the Indians,
> everything was firm land. There were no great liquid masses and
> blue-green shifting oceans.
>   Yara wept because of the loss of his son. All the tribe, fearful of
> hurting him, accompanied him in his mourning and funereal
> dances. Their chants of sadness rose in macabre diapasons:
> *Ia ia ha vê perá iê mê*
> *Aié ienô vexei corindiê.**
>   Yara obtained respect from all the others since he was the all-
> powerful lord before whose magic the warriors prostrated them-
> selves. He wanted the appropriate ceremonies for the deceased, for
> the one that death had robbed from him. Instead of the usual burial
> they made for his son a prolix Ygaçaba over into the shape of a
> calabash. And thus the body of the deceased was encased. The
> funeral urn was placed in a corner in the shade of leafy trees.
>   It then happened that two woodsmen carried away the calabash
> in which the deceased rested. Halfway along their way Yara ap-
> peared before them and wrathfully cursed them. Fearfully, they
> dropped the object which they were carrying.
>   The calabash burst open when it fell, and in place of the corpse
> a great deal of water ran out of its center, from which the seas and
> the deep lakes were formed (60:328).

In this tale the images of the terrible father and the punishment
of the son are all clear (60:329).

*Unintelligible survivances of indigenous language.

Minãhoco (The Giant Worm), *Cabeça de cuia* (Gourd-head),
Negrinho da agua (Little Negro Water-boy), and *Bôto* (River-
siren) are myths in which one finds the same material as in the
previous example. Although they deal with water (birth), their entities are masculine, phallic mothers (60:331). For example, let us
examine the myth of the *Cabeça de Cuia* (Gourd-head).

(109) In Piauí this name (Gourd-head) is used to frighten little
children. It refers to an individual who lives in the Parnaiba River.
He is tall, thin, and has long hair which falls down over his face,
and when he swims he shakes it. He makes his tours during the
river's flooding periods and only infrequently during the dry spells.
Every seven years he eats a girl named Maria, but at times he also
devours little children who are swimming in the river. Because of
this mothers prohibit their children from bathing there. There are
men who stop bathing there during flood periods from fear of being
seized by the previously mentioned bewitched individual. He sprang
from a young man who, disobeying his mother, abusing her, and
abandoning his family, was cursed by the mother and condemned
to live in the waters of the Parnaiba River for forty-nine years.
After he will have eaten seven Marias he will return to his normal
state, the spell having been broken. It is said that his mother will
continue to live while he lives in the waters of the river (6:314).

The Evil Mother

The stepmother is a frequent projection of the Evil Mother in
tales of this type:

(110) The stepmother buries her stepdaughter but leaves her
hair above ground. When someone comes to mow the pasture, a
monotonous song is heard coming from the bowels of the earth:
> Sickleman of my father,
> Do not cut my hair,
> My mother combed me,
> But my stepmother buried me . . .

Pôrto-Carrero states that in the symbolism of dreams the pas-
tureland of hills or ravines is associated with the idea of the hair
which covers Venus' mound. This tale may express even a certain
infantile fantasy about the genital organs of the adult woman. The
hair of the buried girl remaining exposed could be the *pubes
lanuginosus* covering which in infantile mentality substitutes for
the penis which the woman lacks (55:140).

Ramos also gives us a summary of this tale. (1) "The poor dead stepdaughter is buried and from her grave she produces a large pasture. (2) At the time when the harvester is coming to cut it, an anguished voice cries out from the depths of the earth asking that her hair be spared. (3) Finally the grave is opened and the girl is found alive" (56:166). According to him this piece has an Afro-Brazilian origin and psychoanalytically expresses the following: (1) the theme of the phallic mother; (2) a symbolic scene of castration with the harvester who is going to cut the pasture which grew from the grave—the pasture (or the hair) symbolizes the pubes and the act of being cut, the act of castration; (3) the triumph over the anxiety caused by the trauma of birth, consubstantiated in the resurrection theme, that is, in the rebirth, in which the stepdaughter or the hero-son are found alive in the grave (56:166).

Cinderella is another tale in the stepmother or cruel-mother cycle. Ramos notes its universality by pointing out by title its best known versions: Borralheira in Portugal and Brazil; Cenicienta or Ventafochs in Spain; Stactopouta in Greece; Cennerentola and Cenerelle in Italy; Aschenbrödel in Germany; and Cinderella in England and North America (57:212). Most important of all, its ending must be noted psychoanalytically. It belongs to those endings in which the stepdaughters or hero-sons "conquer beauty, fortune, and love." In other words, the son (or daughter) inherits the paternal (or maternal) attributes by means of the mechanism of identification (56:166–167).

In the universally known tale of Tom Thumb the Evil Mother is presented in the person of the witch who seizes the hero to eat him. In some versions there is a witch and a wizard simultaneously. This is what happens in "O Pequeno Polegar," a Brazilian version provided by Câmara Cascudo.

(111) There was once a couple who had twelve children. One of these was the size of a thumb and because of this they called him Tom Thumb. Since this family was very poor and at times had nothing to eat they decided to abandon their children in the woods. On hearing the conversation Tom Thumb went to look for some little pebbles on the banks of the river. In the morning the father led them to the woods and said, "Stay here because I am going to cut some firewood."

The children stayed there and the evil father walked back home leaving them there, lost. The children, afraid of the wild beasts, cried, but Tom Thumb calmed them and brought them home by following the little pebbles which he had let fall along the way so as to show him the way home. The father had received some money and having bought some food, grieved, "Ay! My children! If they were only here!"

Tom Thumb, who was with his brothers and sisters on the other side of the door, came in and were embraced by the parents.

Some time later hunger appeared once again, and the parents again considered abandoning the children in the woods. On hearing the conversation, Tom Thumb tried to run out but he found the door closed. He went to the pantry and picked up a few grains of rice. In the morning the same thing happened again, but when he attempted to return Tom Thumb noted that the birds had eaten all the grains. This time they were lost since they did not know the way home. When night fell Tom Thumb climbed a tree and from up in the tree he saw a light. When he came down he gathered his brothers and sisters together and they set out in that direction.

They arrived at a beautiful big house and knocked and asked for shelter. The woman who answered was a giant. She grabbed them and imprisoned them. When the giant arrived he realized what had happened and ordered the children kept for later.

The giantess put them all to bed in a bed near the one in which the giant's daughters were sleeping, each one having a gold crown on her head. When the giant and the giantess were asleep, Tom Thumb took the little caps of his brothers and sisters (and his own) and exchanged them for the crowns on the giant's daughters heads. Waking up in the middle of the night, the giant felt like killing the children, and taking his sword he went to their room. Arriving there in the dark of the night he began to feel their heads, and finding the crowns on the heads of the children, he said, "Gee! I was about to kill my own little daughters!"

He passed his hands over the heads of the daughters and, finding the little caps on their heads, said, "Here they are!" And he struck them with the sword beheading them all. Then the giant went back to sleep.

Tom Thumb woke up his brothers and sisters and they fled in a hurry. In the morning the giantess went to her daughters' room and fainted! The giant, seeing that he had been tricked, put on his seven league boots and set out to find the runaways.

Seeing the danger, Tom Thumb hid in a cave. The giant was very tired and, stretching out near them, he lay down and fell asleep. Tom Thumb very slowly took off the giant's boots and unsheathing his sword, cut his throat. He then put on the seven league boots and set out for the giant's house. Arriving there he called the giantess and told her, "Your husband is a prisoner and sends for his treasure!"

The giantess gave him everything. Tom Thumb carried what he
could and he returned to his brothers and sisters and they all went
home together. He gave his father the treasure and was later named
royal courier because of the seven league boots (5:215–217).

According to Ramos, Pôrto-Carrero had already attempted a psychoanalytical explanation of Tom Thumb. He ascribed a certain
analogy with the phallus, since this tale includes the symbol "finger" and in psychoanalysis the finger has a phallic meaning. Furthermore, Pôrto-Carrero noted that the hero, Tom Thumb, is always the youngest son, the fondled youngest son of the family, the
last one to occupy the maternal belly, where he had no substitute
(56:172. cf. 55:141).

Ramos completes this analysis, adding: (1) its phallic meaning
expresses a desire to acquire the paternal attributes so as to acquire
authority; (2) the isolation of Tom Thumb in the woods evidently
involves themes of castration and punishment; (3) the hero seeks
vengeance on the father or phallic mother, and in struggling
against them, they assume the sinister form of an old witch, an
ogre, or an evil bird, *Ezuzum*. When venegance is complete the
hero recovers his phallic attributes and discharges his heroic role.

Ramos calls attention to Paul Saintyves' exegesis (*Les contes de
Perrault et les récits parallèles*, 1923) of the tales related to the
theme of Tom Thumb. Ramos states that among the many current interpretations, "Saintyves' thesis is the one which approxi-
mates psychoanalytical explanations the most closely" (56:169).
According to it these tales reveal survivals of cyclical initiation
ceremonies such as circumcision.

To prove this Saintyves cites the African equivalent of Tom
Thumb. He is the Semumu of the Bantus who also call him
Sikulumé and Sékholomi according to the collections of Call
Theal, Jacottet, and Junod. In other parts of Africa Semumu is
also Ngemanduma and Mkidech or Mekidech, according to P. H.
Trilles, *Proverbes, légendes et Contes Fang*, and H. Basset, *Essai
sur la littérature des Berbères* (56:170–171; 57:232). The versions
of Semumu are expressions of rites of passage, according to Sainty-
ves. Let us now look at the summation of one of these by Arthur
Ramos.

(112) Ngemanduma was tiny, feeble, and ugly. Only his head

was very large and because of this they called him Little Big Head. One day the children were attracted by the beating of a drum coming from the woods. Ngemanduma warned them not to go there but they did not listen to him. In the distance the noise of drums was heard. The noise was in the house of the ogre Ezuzum. The children went in and this is just what Ezuzum wanted. He began to sharpen his knife to kill them and to fill the pot with boiling water to cook them. But Ngemanduma came and saved all of them, taking advantage of the moment when Ezuzum had gone to the hill to get firewood. The children set the house on fire. Ezuzum ran back but the roof collapsed on him, and he was burned to death while the children sang:

> Ah! Ah! Ah! Lookey, oh, lookey!
> The fire grilled fat Ezuzum,
> The fire killed fat Ezuzum,
> The fire burned fat Ezuzum,
> Ah! Ah! Ah! Lookey, oh, lookey, oh!
>
> The fire ate him up, kree, kree, kree!
> The one who wanted to eat us up!
> Where's his long knife, the water, and the pot?
> Ah! Ah! Ah! Let's laugh.
> Thanks to Ngemanduma (56:170–171).

Its explanation, according to Saintyves, is as follows. (1) The initiate (the hero), after circumcision, is obliged to retire to a deserted place in the woods. (2) There he has to demonstrate his adolescent valor, he has to pass difficult tests to acquire the privileges of a male in the tribe (in the tale the greatest danger is Ezuzum). (3) But the initiate is successful, even against the greatest danger. (4) The wild imagination of the people exaggerates this success in the most difficult test, adding to it other heroic performances such as the saving of some children, his "brothers and sisters" (56:170).

The important thing is to make it clear that according to Saintyves' thesis the tales in the cycle of Tom Thumb are copies of African initiation ceremonies. These tales unconsciously copy and reproduce these ceremonies.

Applying Saintyves' thesis to the Brazilian version of Tom Thumb (O Pequero Polegar), we would then have the following: (1) Tom Thumb the hero is brought to the woods with twelve children. (2) He succeeds in bringing them back, the preliminary test. (3) He is brought to the woods a second time to face greater dangers. (4) His real epic begins here. He first craftily overcomes force by merely exchanging some crowns. He quickly flees, bringing his charges (his trophy) with him. But he is hunted as he flees, and hunted by a hunter who strides seven leagues with each step. The hero can not cope with this, he can not oppose him; therefore he hides. Then he steals from the giant those things which make him powerful. Having stolen his boots, Tom Thumb identifies with the monster until he is able to outdo him and decapitates him. (5) Final victory. The initiate is received amid rejoicing. He is accepted by his tribe as a man, and is granted honorary titles (royal courier).

In my opinion there is nothing really extraordinary in Saintyves' theory. Its basis is the Tylorian principle or survival which was treated in my *The Concept of Folklore*. This principle is not omitted in ethnological interpretations since it has a high degree of acceptation. We then attempt to identify characteristics of primitive cultures existing in present-day cultures. We know, for example, that totemism and initiation practices (rites of passage, transition rites) are characteristics of primitive cultures. Because of this we speak of totemic survivals and cyclical initiation survivals.

Saintyves' contribution is then similar to that of Nina-Rodrigues who found African totemic survivals in Brazil's folklore; Saintyves found survivals of African initiation rites in certain folkloric tales. They are important as precursors but not as originators since the discovery of totemic and initiation survivals took place in the field of ethnology. Today in Brazil the method for discovering cultural survivals either in folklore or outside of it is common.

We can then appreciate the contribution made by the totemic identification of various folkloric pieces making up the collection of Nina-Rodrigues that is enriched by Ramos. At the same time we see that the latter identified initiatory survivals in some Afro-Brazilian cultural folkloric features.

In the ceremonies of the *yayôs*, or daughters of the saint in the *Candomblés* of Bahia, for example, Ramos found "survivals of these initiation rites for adolescents in religious functions or ceremonies in adult life." (56:175) In some versions of the play about the Congos and the Cucumbis the survivals of the primitive initiation or circumcision were pointed out. In a version recorded by

Mello Moraes Filho, for instance, the Mamêtos (or Princes) were circumcised with a sliver of bamboo (57:64).

Canal-Feijoo in turn found that the legend "Telesita" in Argentine folklore could be the survival of Eleusinian initiation practices. It may be "one of the few subsisting residual indications of marriage practices with a religious basis that has not yet been duly studied by Americanists." It also appears to him that the legends "El Alma Mula" and "De Alma Mula a Condenado" are "probable initiation fragments" in Argentine folklore (7:243, 246:249).

Saintyves' theory did not have to wait long to find supporters. According to Ramos, Alfred Winterstein in Germany showed that European tales and legends repeat the episodes in the transition myths. In these tales, the banished daughters were physically punished or subjected to the care of old women who instructed them on their future duties. This corresponds to the punishment they undergo in order to be able later to endure the pains of childbirth. Ramos adds, "All the primitive rites of puberty express these struggles and preparatory victories of the human function in existence. . . . As for the girl all primitive people oblige her to be completely isolated at the time of her first menstruation. This may last for months or years and be accompanied by severe fasts as well as the prohibition of certain foods (57:233–234).

"Johnny and Mary" is also one of the tales of the worst of the evil mothers. She is an Evil Mother who recalls the one in "Hansel and Gretel" by the Grimm brothers in their famous collection *Kinder und Haus Märchen* (1812), as noted by Câmara Cascudo. The coincidence of additional features between these two pieces is so obvious that "Johnny and Mary" is considered a descendent of "Hansel and Gretel." On the other hand, the analogy between "Tom Thumb" and "Hansel and Gretel" is also so obvious that suspicions exist that one is derived from the other or vice versa. It even occurs at times that separate episodes are taken from these original pieces. These develop their own existence and are used to illustrate very different tales or are then narrated independently. To prove this you need but note *As crianças abandonadas* [The Abandoned Children] and *Botas de sete leguas* [The Seven League Boots].

(113) It is said that once upon a time there lived a very poor

woodcutter who had a large family and they all lived in a little house in the middle of the forest. Even though he worked very hard they were often hungry. One night after supper the wife said that there was nothing left to eat for the following day's breakfast. The husband began to think and finally he said, "It is not worth my having my children with me for them to die of hunger. It would be better to abandon at least two of them on the hill. It may be that they will find a generous soul and that God will have pity on them because they are innocent."

The wife said neither yes nor no but prayed.

Among the children there was a pair of twins called Johnny and Mary. They were very attached to each other. Johnny heard the father's conversation and understood everything. In the morning the woodcutter told them to get dressed and to accompany him to gather wood. Johnny had his pockets full of little white stones from the ground around his house. While they were walking the little boy dropped a stone here or there as a sign. At almost midday the woodcutter stopped and said, "Stay here and rest because I am going to look for some honeybees. When you hear a loud whistle it will be me. Go in that direction."

And he disappeared in the depths of the forest. Johnny and Mary waited a frighteningly long time and heard nothing of the loud whistle. Finally the boy said he was hearing something similar to what his father had said. They went to look for it and found a gourd with its mouth wide open to the wind making the noise. "God bless, we are lost," cried the little girl. "We are going to return home," little Johnny answered.

They started out following the stones and in time, after night had fallen they arrived home. There everyone was eating supper because a creditor paid his bill and there was money for several days. They celebrated and went to sleep.

When the money was all used up and hunger again reared its head, the woodcutter began to think again about leaving the two children in the forest. Johnny could not go out to pick up the white stones because the door was closed and the key was not in the lock. He kept the bread he had received for the road and when he awoke the three of them set out. Johnny fell behind and scattered pieces of bread, but the birds ate them. The same thing happened as the time before. The woodcutter went to hunt bees and when the children went to look for him they only found the big gourd. The little boy wanted to return but he could not find the signs he had left. He became sad but he did not lose courage.

They walked and they walked. When it began to get dark everywhere, little Johnny climbed up in an incredibly big tree. He could see smoke in the distance from up there. He came down quickly and set out leading his sister in that direction.

They found a beautiful house, all lit up inside, and someone singing. Coming closer the two children saw that the house was made of pies and sugared tiles. Johnny broke off a piece which he gave to Mary and he took another for himself. A voice asked, "Who is touching something out there?"

They hid in a hurry but began to eat again. And the voice asked again. The third time they heard the voice very gentle, right at their shoulders, "Ah, so its you my little grandchildren? You're so pretty, but so skinny. Come in."

She was a very ugly old woman, dried up like a broomstick and blind in one eye. She had come up from behind and surprised them eating their fill.

They went in and the old woman, who was a witch, gave them a tasty supper and then led them into a completely empty room. She closed the door and let them sleep. The following day she passed food and water in to them there, and this went on every day. Johnny understood that the old woman ate people and was fattening them up to eat them. He hunted and found a newt and cut off its tail and each time the old woman brought the food and asked how they were, he answered, "We are doing fine." "Show me your little finger!" Johnny would then pass out the newt's tail. The almost blind old woman would feel it and say, "So skinny. Come on, let's eat, my little ones."

And she treated them very well. Months later Johnny and Mary were fat, pink-cheeked, and strong, but still always showing the newt's tail. Unfortunately one time Mary lost the newt's tail and when the old woman asked them to pass out their little finger, Mary, who was guileless, showed her pinky. The old woman felt it and licked her lips, "They are just right. Come on out my little ones."

She let them come out and fed them a rich man's supper. She passed the night making preparations and kneading bread. Early in the morning she woke up Johnny and told him to go outside and fetch more wood. The little boy went outside and saw a pile of wood, cut in sticks. He looked to one side and then the other thinking about what he should do when he heard voices saying, "Little Johnny!" "What?" he answered. "Carry the wood inside and when the old woman lights the large fire and asks you and your sister to cross the board she has put across the middle of it, tell her that it would be better for her to do it first and to show you how to do it. Then push the old woman in the fire and don't pity her."

And so it was. The old woman lit a fire big enough to roast two steers. She put a board across the middle of it and asked the two children to cross to the other side of it. Johnny said that it was dangerous because he did not know how to do it. It would be better if the old woman would show him how. The witch climbed up on the board and when she was exactly in the middle of it, the two of them pushed quickly. The old woman lost her balance and fell in the fire striking the coals and flames and burning herself all over. And she began to scream desperately, "Water, my little ones!" "Oil, granny," they answered. And the old woman was roasted and exploded like a bomb.

Little Johnny and Mary went all over the house and saw the rooms filled with riches, clothes, precious stones, and a great deal to eat and drink.

They took a share of this with them and set out for their parents' home where they arrived several days later. The woodcutter, who had deeply repented, was almost out of his mind with happiness and in tears he embraced his children. The mother's and the brothers' and sisters' joy was beyond words. They all became wealthy and happy. And it began with a duck's foot and ended with that of a chick. My Lord, the King, asked that five be told to me (5:211–214).

Emil Lorenz's German version is an interpretation which Ramos accepted and reproduced. With some slight methodological modifications it is as follows: (1) The children are led into the woods by the parents—the hunger and weaning themes, with the intervention of a cruel mother. (2) The children succeed in returning home, and they lose themselves after their first return—themes which explain an attempt to return to the lost maternal breast. (3) They discover the witch's house. She is going to fatten them up, but the hero shows her a bone and in this way ridicules the witch themes of regression and their dangers. (4) The children throw the witch into the fire, rebelling against her. They later flee and cross the water, assisted by the goose, which is also a regression theme. (5) They return home and are met with affection—which indicates the fixation of the anal phase which follows the oral phase.

Lorenz's final conclusion is that the story of Hansel and Gretel expresses completely a fantasy about weaning. To which Ramos adds, "Psychological weanings take place all through life. And the trauma of renunciation in the phallic phase, is perhaps the strongest of all. It is the one which lasts until the conquest of virility by man and femininity by woman, that is to say, until the complete socialization of the libido" (57:233, 56:174).

The "hero" of Rank (the "son" of Freud) appears indefectibly in the pieces of any of the last groups we discussed, whether they were in pieces in which the totem predominated or in pieces in which the Evil Mother predominated. In our selection we cited no sample where the hero was so engrossing a character as to reach the point of dulling the totem's luster, or the non-totemic Evil Father or Evil Mother. Nevertheless, there are some. Ramos himself points out a path for us by saying, "All the warrior saints were primitive heroes and for this reason, in their religious syncretism, the Brazilian Negroes founded the *Ogun* to Saint Anthony and Saint George as invincible warriors and legendary heroes" (60:345).

Parents, Neither Evil Nor Totems

The psychoanalysis of the African myths about Iemanjá and Xangô helps us to achieve the psychoanalysis of these characters in Afro-Brazilian religions. For this reason and because of the custom of studying Afro-Brazilian culture by comparing it with equivalent cultures in Africa, Ramos studied data on Iemanjá and Xangô from Africa itself. For this he relied primarily on the work of A. B. Ellis, *The Yoruba-speaking Peoples of the Slave Coast of West Africa* (1894).

According to Ellis' records Iemanjá and Xangô exist in Africa in the form of myths and other folkloric species. But in Brazil they are scarce as myths while, on the other hand, they are frequently forms of worship. Concerning Xangô, Ramos confesses, "I have not succeeded in collecting in Brazil any mythical item concerning Xangô." However, he adds that a legend was at least preserved by João do Rio in 1904 (57:22).

Here is the Iemanjá of the Yoruban mythology:

(114) Obatalá the Sky was joined with Odudua the Earth and from this union Aganjú and Iemanjá were born, being respectively Land and Water. Iemanjá married her brother Aganjú by whom she had a son Orungan. The latter fell in love with his mother and began to pursue her until one day taking advantage of the father's absence he violated her. Iemanjá began to run, pursued by Orungan, who proposed living with her. He was about to reach her and put his hands on her when Iemanjá fell to the ground on her back. Then her body began to dilate, to grow disproportionately, until her breasts released two streams of water which joined and formed a large lake. Her belly split open and the following Gods came out of it: (1) Dada, God of the vegetables; (2) Xangô, God of thunder; (3) Ogun, God of iron and war; (4) Olokun, God of the sea; (5) Oloxá, Goddess of the lakes; (6) Oyá, Goddess of the Niger River; (7) Oxun, Goddess of the Oxun River; (8) Obá, Goddess

of the Obá River; (9) Orixá Okô, God of agriculture; (10) Oxóssi, God of the hunters; (11) Oké, Goddess of the hills; (12) Ajê Xaluga, God of wealth; (13) Xapanam (Shankpanna), God of small-pox; (14) Orun, the sun; (15) Oxú, the moon (60:318–319).

In his psychoanalysis, Ramos considers the following elements: (1) In the first place, in this Yoruban myth the Oedipus situation is clearly delineated—the incestuous love of the son for his mother. (2) As to birth of the gods from the mother's belly, this deals with one of the infantile fantasies about birth. He adds that the fantasy in question, that of birth by splitting open of the body, was studied by Otto Rank in his *Völkerpsychologische Parallelen zu den In-fantilen Sexual-Theorien* (1922) (3). The death of Iemanjá must not surprise us. She was a counterpart of Oedipus and was punished for the crime of incest, although the one who should die is the son, punished by paternal anger. What is given here is nothing more than a detour, a disguise, a weakening which Ramos states is common in myths in Rank's judgment (60:319–320).

In Brazil Xangô is an *orixa* or fetishist saint of Yoruban origin. In addition, this word refers to the fetishist religion itself and at times even to the place of worship (57:19).

One of the primitive myths recorded by Ellis in Africa concern-ing Xangô states that Xangô is the second son of Iemanjá and that he came directly out of her body just as we have seen. Ramos adds that in a second version Xangô is the son of Obatalá who had married his three sisters: Oyá, Oxum, and Obá.

(115) One day Xangô received a powerful charm from his father. He tasted it and gave it to his wife Oyá to eat. The following day when Xangô began to speak before the chiefs' meeting in his palace, flames began to spring from his mouth, spreading terror among all so that they fled terrified. Xangô, convinced that he was a god, called his three wives and struck the ground with his foot, which opened up to receive them. Since then he was raised up to the category of an *orixá* (57:21; 60:336).

A third version relates that Xangô was the King of Oyó.

(116) He was the King of Oyó, capital of Yoruba, but he be-came so cruel and tyrannical that the people could no longer stand him. They frightened him into leaving the palace with his three

wives. Xangô challenged public opinion and was deposed. Then he fled by night to Tapa, the land of his mother, accompanied by one of his wives. Then, however, his wife abandoned him and he found himself alone with one slave in the midst of a horrible forest. He asked the slave to return and to wait for him. A long time passed and the slave saw that Xangô did not appear. So he set out to meet him and he found him hanging from the branch of a tree. He returned to *Oyó* to bring them the news, which frightened them all since no one wanted to be responsible for his death. The chiefs came out to meet his corpse, but no one could find it because Xangô had disappeared in the bowels of the earth from which his mournful voice could be heard. They then erected a temple on the site exclaiming, "Xangô is not dead, he has transformed himself into an *orixá*." And since many did not believe this Xangô became violently angry and unleashed a frightening storm filled with thunder and lightning on the city" (60:338–339; 57:21).

According to Ramos these themes contain the components of the Oedipus complex, some clear, others more disguised, but all containing a strong dynamogenic power making the *orixá* an unmistakable image of revolt and fear (60:336). He evaluates separately each one of the mythical examples mentioned. Concerning the second one he avers, "The incest theme in this myth is transferred to his sisters, but in reality this is nothing more than a disguise of the Oedipus theme." (2) The fact that Xangô obtains a powerful charm from his father is a symbol of castration. The son castrates the father and on possessing the charm (phallus) becomes as powerful as he was. "The paternal penis is the magical object par excellence in primitive magical-religious practices, as Roheim has proved in several works. The winning of royalty and divinity are in reality a phallic victory. The son wants to acquire royalty; therefore he steals the paternal attributes. This is what Xangô did, he took possession of the 'magical charm' to transform himself into a god" (60:337–338).

Concerning the third example, he writes, "Psychoanalytically the myth can be translated thus: (1) Xangô who became so powerful because he stole the paternal attributes (the phallus) must be punished. He loses himself in the forest, the magical zone, where the ordeal of his punishment is going to begin. (2) He commits suicide, that is to say, the superego rises violently against the ego and eliminates it in self-punishment for the crime of castration. (3) Xangô disappears into the ground, and once sacrificed, redeems himself and recovers his phallic attributes and changes himself into the *orixá* of thunder and lightening, fire being a very well-known symbol in psychoanalysis."

For greater clarity he adds, "We have here (in this myth) the theme of the resurrected god after the descent into hell which Reik applied to the psychoanalytical problem of Jesus. In this deification of Xangô there is even found the feeling of collective guilt expressed by his subjects. Nobody wants to be responsible for his death. Because of this they erect a temple to him and proclaim his divinity. It is the ancient theme of the deification of the one who sacrifices himself in a holocaust at the collective remorse for the death of the father. In turn it originates a new feeling of imperfection which is the origin of religions" (60:339–340).

Ramos completes his psychoanalysis of Xangô and focuses on him primarily as a hero, closely examining the symbolism which is most suitable to him—fire. "In African myths, and primarily that of Xangô, we have all the episodes of deification of the hero and his substitution for the goddess mother. The primitive father who earlier deified himself does not become clearer, but we have an approximation of the theme in the neglect of the primitive gods and the return of the deified father *orixá-lá*, the king who became a divinity." On the other hand, Xangô having emerged from the waters of Iemanjá's belly expresses a reaction against the trauma of birth. And the fact that he disappears into the earth signifies his return to uterine life since the earth is also a symbol for the mother. In the final analysis, Xangô is the phallic hero of the matriarchal system, of the phase of the goddess-mothers. He then ascended to the category of *orixá* with the disappearance of this matriarchal system (60:344).

Concerning the symbolism of fire evident in Xangô, we must remember that he is the god of thunderbolts, of thunder and lightning, from whose mouth flames shoot out. We have to resort to classic works such as Abraham's *Traum und Mythus*, Rank's *Der Mythus von der Geburt des Helden* and Jung's *Transformations and Symbols of the Libido*. Using these sources, Ramos establishes the following principal points. (1) Fire is libido. Even the expression "the fire of love" so used by poets of all time proves this. (2) The act of lighting the fire symbolizes the sexual act. In India, for example, they represent the former by the picture of coitus. (3)

Jung broadened the sexual meaning of fire, changing it into the source of life itself. (4) By extension, everything else that represents it or can generate it has the same characteristic as fire: flashes, iron, etc. Ramos states that this is why the fetishes of some phallic *orixás* are pieces of iron (60:346). Fire then guarantees Xangô his phallic personality, a personality reinforced by his heroic-mythical adventures and by the content and development of his worship and ritual.

9

The Castration Complex
and Anxiety

Rank considers anxiety the unconscious recollection of the end of the happy uterine existence. Each situation which recalls this primitive past in the life of the individual carries implicitly with it the germs of anxiety. Consequently Rank's theory explains those infantile phobias produced by narrow and dark places. These awaken anxiety because they are analogous, in their darkness, to the maternal uterus and the asphyxiating perils of birth.

Using Rank as a point of reference Ramos finds the explanation for infantile anxiety in the Afro-Brazilian tales of the Kibungo cycle. He states, "The people are imprisoned either in the hole in Kibungo's shoulder, or in the toad's belly, or in the old man's bag. These closed spaces symbolize the maternal uterus. The individuals stay imprisoned there, but at least they are taken out alive. The latter represents an infantile fantasy about birth and a reaction against the trauma of birth which is related to the myths about the birth of the hero" (57:288).

Freud modifies Rank's theory. He reasons that there is no sense in explaining as a reaction to the perception of an analogy, the fear which a child shows on seeing an animal either come out of or go into a hole, since the child can not realize such an analogy. On the other hand, the child should feel happy in the dark since this is nothing more than a restructuring of the intrauterine situation. Nevertheless, he reacts against it with anxiety (28). Freud's theory establishes that anxiety is an affective state which is reproduced each time that the loss of a beloved object (the mother) is thought of. There is the anxiety of birth, since being born signifies loss. The child loses the mother. This loss becomes progressive across the years with successive but measured discharges of anxiety.

Everything that this sensation of loss—of imminent danger—awakens, brings with it the possibility of stimulating infantile anxiety. This is why many folkloric tales appear under the label of anxiety since they are expressions of the child's anxious fear. At the same time, once they have been created, they turn against their creator, this poor autosuggestible being.

We have seen how Freud, under his concept of anxiety, found it in situations of solitude for the child, of substitution of the mother by strange persons, and of threats of castration. Consequently this opens the way for us to the understanding of the tales about monsters, witches, vengeful mothers, stepmothers, and hags. (57:230). These folkloric entities in the field of psychoanalysis correspond to the Evil Father, and the Evil Mother. They are all limitless sources of anxiety because they point out situations of danger or of loss. And to the extent that they are utilized as esthetic projections for children, they become a matter on which educators should take a firm stand.

The Evil Father and the Evil Mother are representations inspired by the substitution of the beloved mother by strong individuals or by the threat of castration before the Oedipus crisis. The child constructs a paternal image in the likeness of an Evil Father whom he castrates and by extension kills. The maternal image is one of the Evil Mother blamed by the daughter for her lack of a penis; she is an assassin, even a devouring mother. In her recent study *Maternidad y sexo*, Marie Langer undertakes to demonstrate clearly that this is a psychological reality. In fact, all of us carry, next to the image of the Good Mother, another horrible one, the image of a mother who kills, destroys, and devours the child. (46:98) When one becomes ill with this complex, he can identify with the Evil Mother of his infancy, even become a delinquent.

A large part of the folklore in the cycle of infantile fantasy in Brazil is primarily of African origin. Gilberto Freyre states, "The African contingent was united with the contributions of the Indians and the Portuguese and provided a large inventory of fears." And he cites as the most threatening, castrating cannibals of the northeast: the *coca* (bogy), *papão* (bogey-man), *lobisomen* (werewolf) *Maria da Manta* (Devilish Mary), *homem das sete dentaduras* (the man with seven sets of teeth), *almas penadas* (suffering souls), *homem-marinho* (merman), *saci-pererê* (one-legged Negro boy), *caipora* (phantom of the woods), *homem-de-pés-às-avessas* (the man with his feet on backwards), *boitatá* (fiery serpent), *mula-sem-cabeça* (headless mule), *negro do surrão* (bogeyman), *mão-de-cabello* (hairy-handed man), *sapo cururu* (fat toad), *os cresce e míngua* (the feast and famine), *papa-figo* (bogeyman), *Kibungo* (a bogeyman with a hole in his shoulders), *Cabeleira* (the hairy one). Others are less popular and cannot be explained in few words: *olharabos, cocaloba, farranca, tango-mango, cabra-cabriola, tutu-marambá, tatu-gambeta, chibamba*. The list is extensive and this page of Gilberto Freyre's is delightful in synthesis and beauty (35:II, 524). Ramos was quite taken with its enchantment and transcribed part of it in his *Folklore negro do Brazil: Demopsicologia e psicanálise*. For extensive studies on the majority of these, refer to Cámara Cascudo's study *Geografia dos mitos brasileiros*. (6) Cascudo dedicates an entire chapter to the myth of horror, calling it "The Cycle of Infantile Anxiety."

As we have noted, the castration complex is intimately related to the Oedipus complex. Consequently many of its folkloric examples were already treated in the previous chapter, specifically in those pieces cited where the Evil Father or the Evil Mother predominated.

Returning to these pieces, let us now point out the characteristics of anxiety created by the threat of castration. Concerning *mano de cabelo*,* for example, Gilberto Freyre expresses himself this way, "The Brazilian myths that involve the suggestion or the threat of castration are numerous." Concerning this he recalls in his *Casa Grande e Senzala* the myth of the merman—the frightening devourer of people's fingers, noses, and genitals (35:II, 524). Ramos has no doubts about its implications concerning the complex in question. The same is true for "The Flabby Toad"** which perhaps has an African origin and is overflowing with infantile anxiety (57:228).

And how can we overlook Pôrto-Carrero whom we have already mentioned? Using Rank's ideas, he refers to the following examples of the castration complex: Cronus who castrates Uranus,

*See example (104).
**See example (105).

his father, and afterwards out of fear of his own children, devours them one by one; Osiris is also castrated, as was Pelopus, who also lacked a homoplate (55:139).

In Tom Thumb* we already observed the theft of the paternal attributes by the hero (the seven league boots) and the paternal castration (the decapitation). As Ramos notes, the head in psychoanalysis is almost always a phallic symbol. This even explains why Tom Thumb is called at times "O Pequeno Cabeçudo" (Little Hard-head) (56:173).

In a word, every time our unconscious ambivalence toward the father makes us hate him, he acquires aspects of a persecutor in our representations. We construct images of Evil Fathers or Evil Mothers of him. We fear being castrated and being robbed. He will steal our penis by castrating us or he will steal our mother. The feeling of loss incites anguish. By extension the father who castrates can devour. The list of cases of the castration complex and of anxiety is filled with devouring fathers, that is, with castrators. They are filled with representations which motivate anxiety and are also stimulated by it in turn.

*See example (111).

10

Infantile Fantasies About Birth

We already know that the child, lacking objective ideas on fecundation and birth, develops fantasies about these matters. These are fantasies which become traditionalized, popularized at times, in a word, folklorized. The most famous paradigm of this kind is the classical stork, a legend which the adults generally keep up so as to free themselves from infantile questions and embarrassing answers. But the stork's story succeeds only in being the least convincing of all to children. They believe themselves closer to the truth with those who believe that birth occurs through the anus or through the navel, or through enigmatic but simple laparotomical surgery.

It is possible to obtain an idea of the universality of the folklore of birth by consulting works on comparative folklore such as Luis da Câmara Cascudo's monumental *Contos Tradicionais do Brasil*. After reproducing "O macaco e a negrinha de cêra" [The Monkey and the Little Wax Negro Girl], Cascudo advises us about the countless versions of the same theme in universal folklore. These versions can then play a role in the folklore of infantile fantasies on birth so long as they contain food and defecation or explosion through the belly. For example the tale "Muhatu Uasema Mbiji" from Loando about a woman who wanted some fish, included in the *Folk Tales of Angola* by Heli Chatelain (5:264).

The African myth of Iemanjá can be used by the reader in this category. As we have already related, several gods are born from Iemanjá's belly when the latter bursts open.*

*See example (114).

The "King of the Birds" falls in this category too. Here is the sequence of its thematic elements. The man (or the woman) wants to eat a bird (or fish). There are protests, warnings, "don't eat me," etc. The animal is eaten and the belly bursts open (explodes), or the animal comes out from the anus. Ramos adds, "The psycho-analytical explanation is as follows. (1) The animal is a symbol of the penis which is going to fertilize the one who ingests it in accordance with the infantile fantasy of fecundation through the mouth. (2) Censure and repression are evident in the animal's warnings and protests. But the penis is eaten in this imaginary fellatio, and fecundation occurs. We then see two final themes. (3) The punishment theme (the person who eats the bird or the fish falls dead in some versions) (4). And the infantile fantasy of birth through the anus which Rank studied extensively in both ancient mythology and plebeian tales" (56:164–165).

(117) A man went out to hunt. Arriving in the woods he saw a very beautiful bird. When he was aiming at it with his carbine, the bird sang:

> "No, no, don't kill me,
> tango-lango-lango,
> 'Cause I'm the King of the Birds,
> tango-lango-lango
> Making yourself my friend
> tango-lango-lango
> Now I *carango**
> tango-lango-lango."

The hunter paid no attention, however. He shot and killed the bird. Arriving home, he told them to prepare the bird to eat. When they began to pluck it, it sang,

> "No, no, don't prepare me, etc."

After it was prepared, they began to cut it into pieces to put it in the pan. It then sang,

> "No, no, don't cut me, etc."

They threw it in the pan, and the bird said,

> "No, no, don't cook me, etc."

And once it was cooked they put it on the plate and the man sat down at the table to eat it. Then the bird sang,

> "No, no, don't eat me, etc."

After the man had eaten his fill, he stretched out and exhaled an "Ah" of pleasure. This was when the bird exploded inside his

*Another Brazilian word which has lost its intellective meaning.

belly—BANG! . . . and flew out. The man fell back dead (48:213; 57:183).

"Pau-piá" is similar to the "King of the Birds."

(118) One day a man went hunting. He put his gun on his shoulder and went into the woods. When he arrived there he saw a very pretty black bird perched on a tree trunk. He readied the gun and was about to shoot when the bird began to sing this song:

> "*Pau-piá,*
> No, no, don't kill me now
> *Pau-piá*
> let me first sing
> *Pau-piá*
> then you can kill me
> *Pau-piá*
> And now, yes!"

The man was greatly astonished by this song, but he paid no attention to it and BANG he shot the bird and it fell dead. How surprised he was then when, on going to pick it up the bird began to sing again,

> "*Pau-piá*
> no, no, don't pick me up now.
> *Pau-piá*
> let me first sing
> *Pau-piá*
> Then you can pick me up,
> *Pau-piá*
> And now, yes!"

Then the man picked him up and carried him home and told his wife to cook him to eat. The wife prepared the pan and was about to put the bird on the fire when the latter began to sing:

> "*Pau-piá*
> No, no don't cook me now.
> *Pau-piá*
> Let me first sing, etc . . ."

After the bird was prepared the man was going to eat it but the latter began again:

> "*Pau-piá*
> No, no don't eat me now, etc . . ."

The man ate it thinking that he was now through with him and that song. Later when he went to defecate the bird sang again:

> *Pau-piá*
> No, no, don't eject me now, etc . . .

When he reached "now, yes!" a quantity of little black devils was seen coming out, jumping and singing (57:185–186).

Since this piece is similar to the previous one the same psycho-analytical data can be applied to it (56:164). The story of "The Monkey and the Little Wax Negro Girl" is another example of the same type as the two preceding ones.

(119) The monkey would go out every day selling his cream so as to have some change to buy himself some dainties. There was a girl who was then his client. What did the monkey do one day? He prepared a pan and put filth in it. He covered the pan with a nice clean towel, and he went out there with the pan on his head. He went straight to the girl's house. When he arrived there and the girl was coming close to him with her cup for the cream, he spilled the filth all over her, did a pirouette, and went down the street splitting his side with laughter, "Kee-kee, kee-kee-kee . . ." The girl was all dirty, smeared, and very angry. She said, "You wait, monkey, until I catch you!"

She ordered a little wax Negro doll made, a doll with a pipe in its mouth, and she put it in the front door. Some time later when the monkey was passing the girl's house he saw the little Negro girl. He came close to her and said, "Little black girl, will you let me smoke your pipe?" The little Negro girl was silent. "Little black girl, let me smoke your pipe, or I'll give you a slap!"

The little Negro girl did not answer, and he—BANG!—gave her a slap and his hand was stuck in the wax. "Little black girl turn my hand loose or I'll give you another slap!" The little Negro girl was silent. He gave her another slap and his other hand became stuck. "Little black girl turn my both hands loose or I'll kick you!" He kicked her and then he had one of his feet stuck in the wax. He gave her another kick and both of his feet stuck. Finally he struck a blow with his head and his head also became stuck. Then the girl had him caught to be killed and eaten. When they were killing him he began to sing,

"Kill me slowly,
'Cause it hurts, hurts, hurts.
Ouch, ouch, ouch,
It was a girl I saw."

He did the same thing when they opened him, quartered him to put him in the pan, when they turned him over, and when they put him on a platter. All of this without it bothering the girl in any way at all. She sat down at the table and began to eat him, and the monkey continued to sing,

"Eat me slowly, etc."

When the girl got up from the table the monkey began to say from inside her stomach,

"I want to come out . . ."
"Come out through my ears."

"I won't come out through your ears because
there is wax in them."
"Come out through my mouth."
"I won't come out through your mouth because
there is saliva in it.
"Come out through my nose."
"I won't come out through your nose because
there is snot in it."
"Come out through the little hole."
"I won't come out through the 'little hole'
because it has s--t."
Finally he exploded, split open the girl's belly and she fell dead and
he nimbly ran outside whistling. "Twee, twee, twee-twee-twee"
(48:185–187).

The Angolese tale of "Kimalaueza of Tumba Ndala," recorded
in Africa by Ladislau Batalha in the original *Kimbundo* is composed of themes similar to those contained in "The King of the
Birds," "Pau-piá," and "The Monkey and the Little Wax Negro
Girl." The analogy was made by Arthur Ramos in *O folklore negro
do Brasil*. He reached the same psychoanalytical conclusions concerning Kilamaueza as he did on the above Afro-Brazilian totemic
tales. The only thematic difference is that in the Angolese tale
the object eaten is neither a bird nor an animal but a fish. This
difference, however, does not alter the psychoanalytical exegesis
since birds, animals, and fish are phallic symbols. The fish as a
phallic symbol is even studied by Otto Rank in his *Völkerpsychologische Parallelen*, which Ramos has consulted (56:164).

(120) "It was said that Mister Kimalaueza of Tumba Ndala, lived
for many years with his wife. Finally she conceived. But she did
not eat meat and preferred to eat fish. When the husband went
fishing he always caught many fish. The latter decided then to
flee to another river. Then the man told his wife, "Fix my meal!"
    The wife did so and he went to the river to which the fish had
fled and stayed there eating. When he finished he said, "Well now,
I'm going to fish!" And he threw his net in the water. The first
time he did not catch anything. The same thing happened the
second time. But the third time the net felt heavier and he heard a
voice from inside the river which said, "Wait, because this friend of
yours is the father of a family." He waited for a long while until he
again heard, "Pull it in now!" He pulled a very large fish out of
the water, threw it on his shoulders, and began to walk away.
    All the fishes accompanied the man, and from the pasture voices

were heard saying, "Ualala! Ualala!" (a shout of admiration, according to L. Batalha). When he reached the house his wife came
out to meet him with all the neighbors. He entered his shack and
gave his wife the fish to cook. His wife told him to scale it and he
replied, "I don't want to!" The wife had to scale it and the fish
began to sing as follows,

> "If you are scaling me,
> Scale me well."

When she finished the chore she put him in the pan, but he continued to sing constantly. When the stew was ready she set five
plates and invited the husband and the neighbors, but they all
refused. As a result she decided to eat alone.

After she finished she stretched a mat out on the ground and
picked up her pipe. But she heard a voice inside her belly which
asked, "By the way, am I going to get out?" She answered, "Come
out through the soles of my feet." The voice again asked, "Am I to
come out through the soles of your feet with which you usually step
in filth?" Again the woman answered, "Come out through my
mouth!"

"Am I to come out through the mouth which ate me?" And the
woman answered, "Come out anywhere you want to!" Then the
fish replied, "Well here I come!" And the woman exploded in
half. But the fish went away (57:188–190).

In *A psicologia profunda ou psicandlise* Pôrto-Carrero refers to
several other selections in which infantile fantasies of birth can
be observed. They are worth recording and preserving as items in
the folklore of fertilization and birth.

Contained in the first group are: Sargon placed in a safe at the
mercy of the waters; the Virgin Mother of Christianity fertilized
by the divine spirit (the spirit equating with a puff, a breath) like
the Greek belief that the winds fertilize the sacred waters, or like
Buddha's mother who was also a virgin; Zeus begetting Athena by
himself, that is, the father begetting without copulation; the
golden egg of Brahma giving birth to the seven Richis, like the
lotus flower from which the Egyptian God Ra sprang; Zeus fe-
cundating Danae with a golden rain (urine).

In the second group we find: the legend of Jonah vomited by a
whale; Little Red Riding-Hood devoured by a Wolf and reborn
through laparotomy; Leda's egg giving birth like the egg of Brahma; the queen who ate monkey excrement as butter and defecated
little monkeys (55:137–139). Bastide also discusses the dwelling as
a sociological example of the trauma of birth (4:80, 97–98).

11

Symbolism and Psychic Mechanisms

On more than one occasion we noted very significant symbolic features and principally as they related to some taboo in the examples we cited. According to Porto-Carrero this sexual symbolism even appears in folkloric selections which deal with the phenomena of nature. It may be that these selections constitute the origin of the interpretation of natural events by primitive man. But above all, it must be observed that they are loaded with sexual symbols. They are attempts at interpretation directed by the libido, "It is through the sexual elements of the fantasies of infancy that primitive man interprets natural phenomena," states Pôrto-Carrero (55:142). According to him "A tapera da lua" [The Moon's Cover] and "Como a noite nasceu" [How Night Was Born], legends from the Indian folklore of Brazil, are found to have such meanings.

The first folkloric records of the legend about the moon's cover were made by Charles Frederick Hartt and Barbosa Rodrigues in the last century. There later appeared two very well known esthetic projections based on these records: the poetry of Mello Moraes Filho in his *Mitos e Poemas* in 1884 and Affonso Arinos' composition in his *Lendas e tradições brasileiras* in 1917. Câmara Cascudo recently clarified these for us in 1952 by translating and commenting on the famous Amazonian tortoise myths by Hartt (38:69). Pôrto-Carrero used A. Arinos' version. Here is Hartt's original from the chapter concerning the "astronomical myths" of the Amazon.

(121) Dr. Coutinho found a myth about the moon in Rio Branco. It was represented by a young lady. She fell in love with one of her brothers and visited him at night. Finally she was betrayed because he passed a hand covered with a black substance over her face. The

same myth was discovered along the Jumanda River by Barbosa
Rodrigues (38:32).

Let us now look at the literary quality of Affonso Arinos' version:

(122) At the time when the Amazons still lived along the banks
of this great river, there was a tribe of Indians whose town was next
to a quiet lagoon along the slope of a range of hills then known as
Tapere, and today Acuna.

An unfortunate war reduced the tribe to two survivors, a brother
and a sister, the handsomest specimens of their race. They were left
alone on the top of the mountain. Then the sister said to the
brother:

"Oh my dear brother! Since you are a man and strong, you will
remain here on the crest of Tapere while I go down to our town
along the banks of the lagoon. I set up your hammock among the
chestnut trees and I left my beautiful arrows alongside of it. The
flowers on the vines which grow along the branches will sweeten
your dreams with their perfume. Good-bye!"

"Good-bye until when?"

"Until the song of the most beautiful birds awakens you by the
morning's light." And with uncertain steps the Indian girl went
down, her eyes sad like those of a wounded doe. By her strange
pallor she showed the weight on her heart.

At nightfall the boy, with his athletic adolescent body, rocked
in the primitive hammock, decked out with many colored plumes
that bristled with the rays of the setting sun. Night fell and already the nighthawk had left his lair when the girl, trembling,
panting, and led on by a strange power, sought the path to the
hilltop looking for the hammock stretched out among the chestnuts.

> She felt love! It was at that moment,
> All alone in the midst of nature,
> That she heard the forest secrete the wind,
> The star to the waterfall.

No one will know this, the secret of my anguish, she breathed. I
will love him in the darkness, and in the daylight I will be his
sister.

> When at the hammock she arrived, the light breeze
> Of the clove whispered through the blinds;
> Darkness in the heavens, palid palpitations,
> Leaps in the bush by the agile guinea-pigs . . ."

And she touches the hammock . . . the hammock trembles. "Who
is it?" She whispers a kiss . . . and the voice dies.

Three times the Indian girl in love climbed the mountain and three times she returned to the deserted town, hiding in the solitude and the darkness of night the secret of her criminal love. But the last time the young Indian man, wishing to unmask the mystery, used a trick. He painted his face with dye from the annatto and the jenipap which grew there to mark the face of the cautious visitor at her first kiss.

And in her town when the sun arose, along the banks of the lagoon, the young lover went to look at herself in the mirror of the waters. Horrors! She saw the black marks of her crime on her very own face.

Then she ran to her bow, took her fighting arrows, and shot the first one toward the sky. Another followed it, and another, and another, and—miracle of the spirits who live in the blue mountains —a long fantastic chain was formed like a staircase of flowers inviting her to climb into the firmament.

She climbed up and was transformed into the moon. Since then, sad and solitary, traveling through space she looks at herself in the waters of the lagoon, in the current of the rivers and in the waves of the sea to see if she still has the stains on her face. (55:142–144, 33–35).

Mello Moraes Filho's erudite poetry quoted by Cascudo is reproduced here:

(123) She perched on a bough, which daily throws
A shadow over the blue peaceful lagoon
Dangling, from its height she sees
Through its modest blush, its features blotched.
Taking the rigid bow, the bow made for war,
She shoots an arrow into the sky; and buries it there,
And others more to the astral lights,
Shooting one, then another, and yet more,
Being next to this waving branch of arrows,
She climbs it to the heavens, becoming the shining moon.

Since then in the streams and rivers and seas
In the mirror of the waters, and the palm grove lakes,
The Indian comes to look at herself, at night and
   in her grief.
To discover if the stains, those stains still show
   on her face (38:69).

Citing Paul Sébillot and his *Le Folklore* of 1913, Cascudo adds that this legend also exists among the Eskimos.

(124) The Eskimos say that the moon was visited every night by

a young man. She painted his back to mark him. On finding out her lover was her brother she fled and he chased her. Both were taken to the heavens and she changed herself into the sun.

"The Moon's Cover" is undeniably an etiological legend about the moon. Pôrto-Carrero's psychoanalytical explanation points out the way in which the moon is related to fraternal incest. This legend prompts him to cite the one about Osiris, the sun (phallic symbol), and Isis, his wife and sister at the same time. It also reminds him of the Greek legend about Endimion, the shepherd loved by the moon.

In the past century the etiological legend about night among the Tupi Indians was objectively recorded by Couto de Magalhães. It appears in 1876 in the first edition of *O Selvagem* [The Savage].

(125) In the beginning there was no night; there was only daylight all the time. Night was asleep at the bottom of the water. There were no animals, everything spoke.

It is said that the daughter of the Big Snake married a young man. This youth had three faithful servants. One day he called the three servants and told them, "Go and take a walk, because my wife does not want to sleep with me." The servants went out and then he called to his wife to sleep with him. The daughter of the Big Snake answered, "It is not yet night." The youth said, "There is no night, only daytime." The girl answered, "My mother has night. If you want to sleep with me, send away for it over there by the big river."

The young man called his three servants. The girl sent them to her father's home to bring back a tucuma palm seed. The servants went on their way and arrived at the house of the Big Snake. He gave them a very tightly closed tucuma palm seed and said, "Here it is. Take it away. Careful now! Don't open it or everything will be lost."

The servants went on their way and they heard a noise inside the tucuma coconut which went like this: ten, ten, tzin, tzin, sheee. (Note: When the savages tell this story they imitate the buzzing of insects.) It was the noise of crickets and little toads who sing in the night. While they were still far away one of the servants said to his companions, "Let's see what's making that noise." The pilot said, "No. On the contrary we'll get lost. Let's go now. Row!"

They went on and continued hearing the noise inside of the tucuma coconut seed, and they did not know what was making the noise. While they were still very far away, they got together in the middle of the canoe, lit a fire, and melted the resin which closed the coconut seed and opened it. Immediately everything became dark. The pilot then said, "Now we are lost. And the young lady in her house will know that we opened the tucuma coconut seed!"

They continued on their way. The young girl in the house then told her husband, "They released the night, let's wait until morning." Then everything that was appropriately distributed throughout the woods was transformed into animals and birds.

The things that were scattered along the river were transformed into ducks and fishes. From a baker's basket there arose a tigress. The fisherman and his canoe were changed into a duck. From his head, the head and beak of a duck were born; from the canoe the body of a duck; and from the oars the duck's feet.

When the daughter of the Big Snake saw the morning star she told her husband, "Dawn is beginning to appear. I am going to separate the day from the night." Then she wound up a thread and said to it, "You will be the Amazonian piping guan." Thus she made the piping guan. She painted the Amazonian piping guan's head with colored clay and its feet red with annatto dye and then said, "You will sing for everyone when dawn begins to break." Then she wound up another piece of thread, urinated on it, saying, "You will be a partridge and you will sing during the night and early hours of the morning." And from that time on all the birds sang at their appointed hours and during the early morning to cheer up the beginning of the day.

When the three servants arrived the young man said to them, "You were not faithful. You opened the tucuma coconut and let nighttime loose and everything was lost as you are also. I have transformed you into monkeys and you will walk through the branches of trees forever." (The black mouth and yellow streak on their arms is said to be the mark on monkeys of the resin which spilled on them from the seal on the tucuma coconut seed.) (20:231–234; 55:144–148).

According to Couto de Magalhães the legend expresses such similarity with Asiatic thought that we can even ask if it is not an echo of the same thought. In this tale we need but substitute tucuma seed for the forbidden fruit. This tale is probably a fragment of the "Genesis" of the ancient South American savages.

Pôrto-Carrero discovers sexual symbols in it which are identical to those in myths and dreams. The woman's belly and the phallus appear in it, symbolized respectively by the tucuma coconut seed from which night with its fears and mysteries is born, and the Big Snake and the fire. They opened the tucuma coconut (which reminds us of Pandora's box) with fire and melted the resin which sealed it.

The field of symbolic interpretation is limitless. It occurs not only in ideational verbal folklore (poetic and narrative forms) but also in motor-perceptive folklore (material, ergological folklore, plebeian art, dances, etc.). The feast of *curuzú-yeguá* [guaraní: adorned cross] and the popular art of *ñandutí* are replete with symbols. Dealing with their cultural complexes is the most difficult problem when psychoanalyzing them. To do so requires a considerable body of descriptive folkloric data as a foundation. The *curuzú-yeguá* and the *ñandutí* are treated in detail for the first time in my *Folklore del Paraguay*.

Curuzú-yeguá is the "feast of the cross." It occurs on the sixth of May in all of Paraguay. I attended one of these in the Campamento Loma, a Negro region, and this is a report of the happenings:

> (126) This feast consists of decorating the cross, calling in the neighbors, laughing and dancing, as is the case with feasts in general. But the cross is decorated primarily with *chipas*,* that is, with breads made from manioc flour. These breads are shaped by the women who made them, and when they are ready they are affixed to the cross. They make a considerable quantity of bread which is sufficient for all those who are invited. The cross with these breads is worshipped and the happy noise of a fiesta prevails. Afterwards the meal comes. The cross caretaker divides the bread among those present and they eat it happily and comment on how good it is. But in the distribution of the bread one can choose what one wishes to eat, be it a ladder, a man, or a snake. The breads are molded in these shapes as well as in those of other symbols.

Are not the items which traditionally appear in the *curuzú-yeguá*, the ladder, the man and the snake, for example, perhaps sexual symbols? They are in most dreams, at least. Freud has classified and evaluated them in his table of oneiric symbols in *The Interpretation of Dreams*, (29) and *A General Introduction to Psychoanalysis* (26).

The entire body creates the maximum eroticization. It is the displaced, enlarged penis which is confused with the human whole. The snake is the eroticization of the penis, and the ladder is the symbol of the sexual act itself, rhythmical and ascending.

In the *curuzú-yeguá*, the eating of these symbolic items very

---

*chipas—Name in the Rio de la Plata region for cakes or loaves made of maize, cassava, or manioc flours.

clearly provides a sensation of aggrandizement. This is primarily true when we consider that these symbols are only made during the feast itself although *chipas* are made for commercial purposes every day. My analysis of the *curuzú-yeguá* is supported by many factors which I will try to develop in a schematic way.

1. The *chipa* is made every day in Paraguay for commercial purposes.

2. The symbolic *chipa* occurs principally at the time of the feast of *curuzú-yeguá*.

3. The adoration of the cross is not merely the admiration of the cross; it is also the adoration of the symbolic *chipa*, since on that day one is not adored without the other.

4. The confluence of the symbolic *chipa* with the cross in the same worship is an evident syncretism. This leads us to suppose that at an earlier time there existed only the adoration of the symbolic *chipas* and that the cross was introduced as a Catholic ceremonial disguise due to the power of the Jesuits. This was what Nina-Rodrigues discovered in Brazil while observing the adoration of Christian saints adorned with fetishist pieces which at first glance appear meaningless. This is to say, the Africans in Brazil disguised their worship by introducing Catholic images and thus obtaining permission to meet and worship. This was the "great illusion of catechizing" of which Nina-Rodrigues speaks. In time the saints incorporated the African worship, resulting therefore in a strange Afro-Brazilian syncretism. The cross represents the Christian symbol in the *curuzú-yeguá*. The *chipas* are not Christian but separate symbols which predate the cross.

5. We can even concede that truly primitive fetishes which were destroyed, actually predated the *chipas*. An attempt was made with the *chipas* to reconstruct them. On molding the breads they were unconsciously given the shape of their repressed contents: snakes, ladders, etc., and these symbols became traditional.

This hypothesis is probably quite close to the truth, especially when one considers that other writers such as Goicochea Menéndez and Natalicio González felt that the *curuzú-yeguá* was a survival of the ancient worship of Curupí. And you ask, "Who is Curupí?" He is that mythological entity whose organ was so deformed that it managed to reach around the waist of his little body. This description was reported by a traveler named Aguirre in 1793 (17).

In other words, Curupí is a phallic entity. The hypothesis that the *curuzú-yeguá* is a survival of the ancient worship of Curupí cannot be cast aside at all. In the *curuzú-yeguá* this survival can be verified by the ladder, the snake, the human body, and other symbols of this type. These symbols then represent Curupí. Due to the social impossibility of worshipping Curupí and the pressure of the Jesuits, the Indians—following the example of Catholic clergymen who reproduced their Christian God by bread—did likewise. But the disguise is not complete. They then added the Curupí bread to the cross and achieved "the great illusion of catechesis."

6. Deified Curupí-bread is then eaten by the participants in the ceremony. This is a common cannibal scene in all religions. And afterwards the devout feel strong and pure. The individuals have assimilated the virtues of the god.

7. We must yet ask, "Why did they not choose another Christian feature to put along side of the Curupí bread? Why did they not select anthropomorphical idols instead of the Cross?" It is possible that an explanation may be provided by a more generic imitation of Christianity than had been supposed. After symbolizing Curupí in the *chipa*, as Jesus is in the host, the Indians went one step further and provided for the crucifixion of the symbolic Curupí, similar to what had happened to the Christian Lord. *Curuzú-yeguá* (the adorned cross) becomes the reproduction of the tragedy of Calvary. It becomes the crucifixion of the god Curupí. In the *curuzú-yeguá* the cross is used and the bread affixed to it as if it had been crucified there.

This hypothesis is supported by the fact that the *curuzú-yeguá* must simulate on elevation or a wooded place. For this reason tree limbs, bunches of living hemp-brake, flowers, and stems of roses are placed around it. In 1766 in Paraguay they even went up to the very tall crosses already erected on the hills. There was then no reason to simulate Calvary because these were Calvaries.

Aguirre describes for us the *curuzú-yeguá* of Cerro del Yaguarón. "On the day of the Cross of May, the priest goes up to it and says his prayers at it. They decorate it and place many *chipas* and edibles on it according to the custom of the country" (17). Note how in those days the priest was present. His presence was a further disguise for the Guaranis' worship of Curupí.

The symbolism of the *ñandutí* is worth studying in relation to the *curuzú-yeguá* so that the differences between them stand out. Of course, the *ñandutí*'s symbolism is very different from that of the *curuzú-yeguá*. It is simple symbolism, that is, it is in the first stage of the symbolic process—analogy by graphic similarity. And it does not go beyond this. This is what basically characterizes it. The path from its manifest content to its latent content is short and direct. There are no detours or disguises, and consequently there is no censorship. If there is no censorship or interdiction of its themes it is because they do not contain any incestuous desires. That is, the *ñandutí* is the aggregate of unrepressed, not unconscious symbols. It is like classic art which sketches themes on the landscape which one perceives for esthetic purposes. The weaver in this case spends week after week, month after month, and at times years to achieve a collection of perfect copies.

The conscious and refined esthetic preoccupation is absent in the *curuzú-yeguá*. The symbols are developed in a few moments and at the will of the artist in his creative moment. It is evident that the symbols of the *curuzú-yeguá* do not involve conscious esthetic objectives but rather unconscious psychic objectives which are at the same time more complex. *Ñandutí* can be equated with classical art, measured, faithful to the model, and proportioned. On the other hand, the *curuzú-yeguá* corresponds to modern art, apparently revolutionary, primitive, and incongruent.

If everyone were to make a snake in the *curuzú-yeguá*, each of the snakes would be different because each individual has within him the model for it. It is engraved in his memory. In the *ñandutí* when they all make the *arasapé* (the flower of a guava) this form has to satisfy certain forms common to all *arasapés*. If one departs from these norms in the *ñandutí* it is then said that the job is badly done, and that its acquisitional value is consequently diminished. There are no well made nor poorly made symbols in the *curuzú-yeguá*. They are merely symbols and possess no acquisitional value.

(127) The sun, the *arazá* (Catley guaya) flower, the coconut flower, the corn flower, the barley spike, the bull's tracks, the cat's claws, the goat's tail, the sheep-tick, moth, the sheep, the little bird, the butterfly, and many others are symbols of the *ñandutí* (17).

Under such conditions the symbolism of the *ñandutí* is of far less interest to psychoanalytical folklore than the symbolism of the *curuzú-yeguá*. In the latter the symbolic development is very complex and its corresponding analysis is difficult.

The hypothesis of direct analogy is not convincing in the *curuzú-yeguá* since there is a general lack of meaning to the decoration of a cross with snakes for its worship. It is not the same thing as decorating a chest for its sale. These decorations of the *curuzú-yeguá* have other and hidden meanings. They are complex symbols and their meaning is hidden because they are socially and unconsciously prohibited. And if the mantle of prohibition falls over them they must, in truth, have been greatly desired, almost incestuously desired.

The *curuzú-yeguá* (the manifested folkloric contents) corresponds to the following latent contents: Curupí, who in spite of being socially and unconsciously repressed as a result of being a fervent libidinous desire, continues to be satisfied as a disgraceful item which can not be confessed. But his condition of censored, repressed desire makes him adopt other outward appearances. The snake, the ladder, etc., come from this. The Curupí disguised this way is then placed in other environments, the socially predominant ones, such as, for example, the Christian one of the Cross.

MECHANISMS OF THE PSYCHIC SYSTEM

"The Tortoise and the Lizard" is a Brazilian folkloric tale recorded in 1897 by Silvio Romero in his *Contos Populares do Brasil*. Nina Rodrigues demonstrated its African origin by comparing it with the tale "The Tortoise and the Elephant," recorded in Africa by A. Ellis in *The Yoruba-speaking Peoples of the Slave Coast of West Africa* (1894) (53). At that time Couto de Magalhães, who supported the solarist theory developed by Hartt in his *Amazonian Tortoise Myths*, was searching for totemic Brazilian tales so as to interpret them. Because of this he utilized the example in question. Ramos believes, however, that the solarist theory only makes the problem recede. For him the magical aspect of the tales of the tortoise is evident. The power of the tortoise knows no obstacles in certain tales. She conquers everything in a phantasmagoric way and deceives everyone. In other words, the symbolism is clear, the

emotions must be repressed, restrained, surmounted (56:164). Note
how the principle of reality is interposed with the principle of
pleasure. Censure makes itself felt and repression occurs; the superego corrects the ego.

(128) Once upon a time there was an lynx that had a daughter.
The lizard wanted to marry her and friend tortoise did too. The
tortoise, knowing of the former's claim said, in the lynx's house,
that the lizard was good for nothing, and that he even used him
as a horse. As soon as the lizard found this out, he went to the
lynx's house and assured her that he was going to go out and find
the tortoise, bring him there, and give him a good beating with a
stick in front of everyone, and he left.

The tortoise, who was at home, on seeing him from a distance,
ran inside and tied a handkerchief around his head, making believe
he was sick. The lizard came to the door and invited him to take a
walk to friend lynx's house. The tortoise excused himself at length
saying that he was sick and could not go out on foot that day.
The lizard insisted a great deal. "Then," said the tortoise, "you'll
have to carry me mounted on your back." "Of course," answered
the lizard, "but up to a distance from the door of our friend the
lynx." "Very well, but you'll have to let me put my shell saddle
on you because riding bareback this way is very ugly." The lizard
became annoyed and said, "No, I'm not your horse." At last the
lizard consented. "Now," said the tortoise, "let me put the bridle
on you." A new outburst by the lizard and more requests and ex-
cuses by the tortoise until he succeeded in putting the bridle on
the lizard and fitting himself out with a whip, spurs, etc. They set
out and when they arrived at a place not very far from the lynx's
house, the lizard asked the tortoise to get down and take off the
harness because it would be very bad if he was seen serving as a
horse. The tortoise replied that he had been very patient and to
go a little farther ahead because he was very ill and could not reach
the house on foot. And so he kept tricking the lizard until the lynx's
door where he hit him with the whip and the spurs. Then he
shouted inside the house, "Look didn't I say that the lizard was
my horse? Come and see!" There was a great deal of laughter, and
the tortoise victorious, said to the lynx's daughter, "Come, girl, climb
on my back, and let's go get married." It happened this way to the
great shame of the lizard (57:175–177).

12

Conclusions

Prior to stating my conclusions a brief reference should be made to the phenomena of fetishist possession and epidemic psychosis. An explanation should be provided as to why they were not included in a fictitious "folklore" of hysteria. They are in fact related to hysteria, but not to folklore.

Fetishistic possession is a cultural phenomenon which can be observed in Brazil in the fall of the saint during Afro-Brazilian *candomblés* and *macumbas*. The *filha do santo* (daughter of the saint) falls in a trance and is possessed by strange chorea-like hysterical movements. This state reflects not only a prelogical mentality, as outlined by Lévy-Bruhl, but something more. Pathologically speaking, it is something more—it is insanity, it is hysteria—and because of this it loses its characteristic of being a folkloric manifestation.

The phenomenon of possession in the Middle Ages was noted in those who were possessed by the devil. Exorcists conjured the devil for the Christians while witch doctors accomplished the same thing in the primitive and magical realm. Exorcism and dispatches were fundamentally the same kind of an act.

The entire topic of possession whether by fetishes or the devil has a rather considerable bibliography in both the ethnographic and psychoanalytical realms. Those who have synthesized it in South America are Arthur Ramos in Brazil in his "The Phenomena of Possession" in *The Negro in Brazil* (60) and Nerio Rojas in Argentina in *El diablo y la locura y otros ensayos* (64).

It is interesting to note that the medieval Inquisition burned at the stake not only those who were "possessed by the devil," that

is, those which were in fact hysterical, but they also extended their
judgment as to possession by the devil to those who dealt with
witchcraft, divination, conjuring, philtres, fumigations, and magic
in general. Don Sebastian Cirac Estopañán's contribution, *Los
procesos de hechicerías en la Inquisición de Castilla la Nueva*,
provides clear documentation of this (19).

Charcot's research pointed out the extent of the abnormality
and hysteria contained in these pathologies which are related to
the devil. The Inquisition's concept of the devil had to be sub-
divided. Those who had fits of possession fell into the category of
hysteria. These were disassociated from such categories as magicians, fortune-tellers, witch doctors, etc., even though the Inquisition lumped them all in the category of "possessed."

The entire second group, which is nonhysterical, has passed
into the realm of folklore and primarily into the classification of
narcissism. Those who are possessed by seizures, such as the daughters of the saint, belong in the realm of the psychiatry of hysteria.
Furthermore, we must not forget, as Dr. Nerio Rojas notes, that
there are cases where it is very difficult to separate what is solely
superstition from what is pathological. If the former is a subject
for folklore and is of interest to the sociologist, the latter deals
with clinical observations and is important in psychiatry. Both,
however, explain each other reciprocally (64).

Ramos adds the cases of epidemic psychosis (mass psychosis) of a
religious nature but without possession to those of mass possession
"by the devil" (60). Because of their psychopathic nature both of
these are nonfolkloric expressions of plebeian culture. They are a
part of the study of mass psychology and psychiatry, but not of folklore. They also belong to the classification of hysteria but not to
folklore. They have been classified this way in Brazil by Arthur
Ramos. He pointed out the following studies as forerunners in this
area: Alfredo Brito, *Contribuição ao estudo da astasia-abasia neste
Estado* (1890); Nina Rodrigues, *Abasia choreiforme epidêmica no
norte do Brasil* (1890); Nina Rodrigues, *A loucura epidêmica de
Canudos: Antonio Conselheiro e os Jagunços* (1897); Nina Rodrigues, *Epidemie de folie réligieuse au Brésil* (1898); Nina Rodrigues,
*La folie des foules. Nouvelle contribution à l'étude des folies
épidemiques au Brésil* (1901); Lourenço Filho, *Joazeiro do Padre
Cicero* (n. d.); Xavier de Oliveira, *Beatos e Cangaceiros* (1920);

Xavier de Oliveira, *Espiritismo e loucura* (1931); Gustavo Barroso, *Heróis e bandidos (Os Cangaceiros do Nordeste)* (1917); Gustavo Barroso, *Almas de lama e aço* (n. d.); and Ranulpho Prata, *Lampeão* (1934) (60:267).

It is now possible to begin outlining the principal conclusions of this study of folklore and psychoanalysis, or to be more specific, analytical demopsychology. These concern man, the folkloric act (folklore), and the science of folklore (Folklore).*

Psychoanalysis permits Folklore to characterize the plebeian bearer of a folkloric act as one who is motivated by nonsocialized impulses of his libido, in other words, the primitive impulses of his libido. In this sense Freud's contribution complements Lévy-Bruhl's since the latter characterized primitive mentality (plebeian mentality) as belonging to an individual motivated by mystical or prelogical formulas while engaged in the process of thinking.

While we attempt to understand plebeian folkloric man, psychoanalysis and the recent contributions of Malinowski, Kardiner, and others help us to understand the cultural folkloric act itself and the science of Folklore. It explains the reason for the act and reveals its true significance. Furthermore, analytical demopsychology underlines the normative importance of Applied Folklore.

When considering Folklore as a normative social science (Applied Folklore) we see that it can and must participate in the social order to improve it. It must intervene in an indirect way by criticizing and censuring. It provides criticism for the educators who then implement changes.

As the primitive forms of the libido are studied, it becomes apparent that a portion of this material must continue in force and even be supported by a stream of learned worshippers of tradition. Concerning the other part, however, it is clear that it must end, and it must be eliminated by positive and adequate educational methods.

The usable part is immediately taken over by the traditionalists and the esthetic projectors because of its identification with the ethical and esthetic norms of the elite of the culture. Scientifically speaking, the former are almost always antifolklore. It is also taken

---

*Up to this point I have used *folklore* in lower case to identify both the science and the act. To be more precise, I will now use a capital letter to identify the science and lower case the act.

over by those educators who wish to tighten the bonds of nationalism through folklore.

The useless part is subject to correction by the educational
system and the police. In an ideal plan they attempt to substitute
the latest and most important discoveries of man for superstition,
plebeian medicine, and witchcraft. In this sense then Folklore
brings folklore to an end. The science of Folklore ends up by
eliminating folkloric acts. Finally, it is satisfying to note that
Folklore can assist man to adapt himself to new and better stan-
dards of living by freeing him from fear and from archaic representations. Ramos truly understands this. He studied Folklore to
use its findings in education. Folklore provides evidence that primitive modes of thought exist in a region and the educational structure can then attempt to eliminate them. And this must be performed in depth. The educational task based on discoveries in the
field of Folklore must be vertical and interstitial. It must go to
the most remote corners of the collective unconscious and free the
mind from the prelogical ties which bind it there. Ramos states
that, "All our efforts will be sterile if we do not cast off all the
unconscious snares of error and superstition and prevent a blind
and insidious resistance from later invalidating the dedicated work
of hygenists and educators" (60:31, 30).

Applied Folklore is a liberating discipline. The folklorist is
partially a specialized medical doctor who localizes and diagnoses
a malady so that the surgeon (the educator) can remove it. This
removal consists of replacing prelogical elements by more rational
ones. Ramos indicates that, "Freedom will result from this domination of fear, the domination of this permanent representation of
fear which in the final analysis is related to libidinal anxiety.
Societies possess merit because of the progressive conquests of the
steps in the eroticization of their relations in the psychoanalytical
meaning of the stages of the libido." In other words, "The processes
of the *Almacht der Gedanken* must be substituted by others which
are more logical, more rational, and freer from the underlying emotional amalgam. We must go from narcissism to the complete
socialization of the libido" (60:408, 409).

Finally I feel that the relationship between Folklore and education and Folklore and literature and the fine arts must be clarified even further. Education is concerned with the totality of folk-

lore. One part, the "usable part," is cultivated and developed in the schools and in similar institutions so as to maintain, for example, the bonds of nationalism. As to the useless part, it attempts with police support to suppress it.*

Literature and the fine arts are only interested in the usable part of folklore, a part which they attempt to recreate and fashion more esthetically. In other words, the folklorist is found where collection, classification, comparison, and interpretation may be taking place. The nostalgic evocation provided by folklore characterizes the traditionalist or the esthete—the poet, the literary figure, the musician, and the artist. The diffusion of what is "good" in folklore is the province of the educational field as is also the correction of folklore which is useless. On many occasions the interests of educators will coincide with those of esthetes.

No nostalgic love of the past can interfere with the studies performed by folklorists. Folkloric tradition is studied as a whole, without the ethical or esthetic bias of any elite. A tale or a popular ditty must be analyzed with the same objectivity as an act from "the secret closet of folklore." There must be no sentimental bias toward any side.

A folklorist must not be confused with a traditionalist or an educator. Where a folklorist may be suggesting the development of usable folkloric acts for us he ceases being a folklorist and assumes the role of an educator, an educator specialized in Applied Folklore. A folkloric week, which is characterized by acts evoking the gaucho culture, never merited its use of the word folkloric, since its aims are far from the serious study and research objectives of folklorists—the discussion of a thesis, the discussion of problems touching on the techniques of collection, models of classification, the results of comparison, and the methods of interpretation.

*I later developed this thesis in my *Folklore y Educación*.

Bibliography

1. Angrand, C. and Garaudy, R. *Curso elemental de filosofía.* Translated by Raquel Warschaver. Buenos Aires: Editorial Lautaro, 1947.
2. Arinos, Affonso. *Lendas e tradições brasileiras.* 2nd edition. Rio de Janeiro: F. Briguiet & Cia Editôres, 1937.
3. Barroso, Gustavo. *Ao som da viola. Folclore.* Corrected and expanded edition. Rio de Janeiro: Departmento de Imprensa Nacional, 1949.
4. Bastide, Roger. *Sociologia e Psicoanálise.* São Paulo: Instituto Progresso Editorial, S. A., 1948.
5. Câmara Cascudo, Luis da. *Contos Tradicionais do Brasil. Confrontos e notas.* Rio de Janeiro: Americ Edit., 1946.
6. Câmara Cascudo, Luis da. *Geografia dos mitos brasileiros.* Rio de Janeiro: Livraria José Olympio Editôra, 1947.
7. Canal-Feijoo. B. *Burla, credo, culpa en la creación anónima. Sociología, etnología y psicología en el folklore.* Buenos Aires: Editorial Nova, 1951.
8. Carneiro, Édison. *Candomblés da Bahia.* Bahia: Museo do Estado, 1948.
9. Carneiro, Édison. *Dinâmica do Folklore.* Rio de Janeiro: 1950.
10. Carneiro, Édison. *Negros bantus. Notas de etnografia religiosa e de folklore.* Rio de Janeiro: Civilização Brasileira, S. A., 1937.
11. Carvalho, Ivolina Rosa. "Folklore do Morro das Pedras." Unpublished manuscript.
12. Carvalho-Neto, Paulo de. "Folklore floridense." *Folklore Americano,* 5 (1957), 5–60.
13. Carvalho-Neto, Paulo de. *Folklore y Educación.* Quito: Casa de la Cultura Ecuatoriana, 1961.
14. Carvalho, Ivolina Rosa, et al. "Folklore paraguayo brasileño." Asunción: Comunicaciones del Centro de Estudios Antropológicos del Paraguay, No. 15, 9 August 1951. Mimeographed.
15. Carvalho-Neto, Paulo de. *The Concept of Folklore.* Translated by Jacques M. P. Wilson. Coral Gables, Fla.: University of Miami Press, 1970.

16. Carvalho-Neto, Paulo de, et al. "Fichas de Medicina Popular." Montevideo: Primer Coloquio Uruguayo de Folklore. III Comisión, Doc. No. 12, 1956. Mimeographed.

17. Carvalho-Neto, Paulo de. *Folklore del Paraguay. Sistemática analitica.* Quito: Editorial Universitaria, 1961.

18. Carvalho-Neto, Paulo de, et al. "La Magia en el Uruguay. Contribución al Folklore de Durazno." Montevideo: First Uruguayan Colloquium on Folklore, 1956. Mimeographed.

19. Cirac Estopañan, Don Sebastián. *Los procesos de hechicerías en la Inquisición de Castilla la Nueva.* Madrid: Consejo Superior de Investigaciones Científicas, 1942.

20. Couto de Magalhães, General. *O Selvagem.* 1876; 4th edition, complete with a general course in the Tupi language. Rio de Janeiro: Companhia Editôra Nacional, 1940.

21. Dalbiez, Roland. *Psychoanalytical Method and the Doctrine of Freud.* Translated by T. F. Lindsay. 2 vols. London: Longmans, Green and Co., 1941.

22. Ellis, Havelock. *Psychology of sex: A Manual for Students.* New York: The American Library, 1954.

23. Frazer, James G. *Totemism and Exogamy: A Treatise on Certain Early Forms of Superstition and Society.* London: Macmillan and Company, Ltd., 1910.

24. Freud, Sigmund. *The Ego and the Id.* Translated by Joan Riviere. Revised and edited by James Strachey. New York: W. W. Norton and Company, Inc., 1960.

25. Freud, Sigmund. *Five Lectures on Psychoanalysis.* Authorized translation by James Strachey. Vol. XI, *The Complete Psychological Works of Sigmund Freud.* London: The Hogarth Press and the Institute of Psychoanalysis, 1968.

26. Freud, Sigmund. *A General Introduction to Psychoanalysis.* Authorized translation by Joan Riviere. New York: Washington Square Press, 1935.

27. Freud, Sigmund. "Group Psychology and the Analysis of the Ego." Authorized translation by James Strachey. *The Complete Psychological Works of Sigmund Freud.* London: The Hogarth Press and the Institute of Psychoanalysis, 1955.

28. Freud, Sigmund. "Inhibitions, Symptoms, and Anxiety." Vol. XX, *The Complete Psychological Works of Sigmund Freud.* Authorized translation by James Strachey. London: The Hogarth Press and the Institute of Psychoanalysis, 1955.

29. Freud, Sigmund. *The Interpretation of Dreams.* Authorized translation by James Strachey. New York: Avon Books, 1965.

30. Freud, Sigmund. "New Introductory Lectures on Psychoanalysis." Vol. XXII, *The Complete Psychological Works of Sigmund Freud.* Authorized translation by James Strachey. London: The Hogarth Press and the Institute of Psychoanalysis, 1955.

31. Freud, Sigmund. "On Narcissism: An Introduction." Vol. IV, *Collected Papers*. Authorized translation by Joan Riviere. London: The Hogarth Press and the Institute of Psychoanalysis, 1948.

32. Freud, Sigmund. "Papers on Metapsychology." Vol. XIV, *The Complete Psychological Works of Sigmund Freud*. Authorized translation by James Strachey. London: The Hogarth Press and the Institute of Psychoanalysis, 1968.

32.a. Freud, Sigmund. "Papers on Technique." Vol. XII, *The Complete Psychological Works of Sigmund Freud*. Authorized translation by James Strachey. London: The Hogarth Press and the Institute for Psychoanalysis, 1968.

33. Freud, Sigmund. *Three Essays on the Theory of Sexuality*. Authorized translation by James Strachey. New York: Avon Books, 1962.

34. Freud, Sigmund. *Totem and Taboo*. Authorized translation by James Strachey. New York: W. W. Norton and Company, Inc., 1950.

35. Freyre, Gilberto. *The Masters and the Slaves*. Translated by Samuel Putnam. New York: Alfred A. Knopf, 1946.

36. Garibaldi, Verdad Risso de and Garibaldi, Carlos Alberto. *Cancionero infantil. Canciones, rondas y juegos folklóricos y populares de América y España*. Musical annotations by Prof. Sara Acosta. Montevideo: Departamento Editorial del Consejo de Enseñanza Primaria y Normal, 1946.

37. Glover, Edward. *Freud or Jung*. New York: W. W. Norton and Company, Inc., 1950.

38. Hartt, Charles Frederick. *Amazonian Tortoise Myths*. Rio de Janeiro: W. Scully, 1875.

39. Jijena Sánchez, Rafael. *El perro negro*. Buenos Aires: Ediciones Dolmen, 1952.

40. Jones, Ernest. *What is Psychoanalysis?* New York: International Universities Press, 1948.

41. Jung, Carl G. *Psychology and Religion: West and East*. Vol. II, *Collected Works*. Translated by R. F. C. Hull. New York: Pantheon Books, Inc., 1958.

42. Jung, Carl G. *Psychological Types*. Vol. VI, *Collected Works*. Translated by R. F. C. Hull. New York: Pantheon Books, Inc., 1953.

43. Jung, Carl G. *The Relations Between the Ego and the Unconscious*. Vol. VII, *Collected Works*. Translated by R. F. C. Hull. New York: Pantheon Books, Inc., 1953.

44. Jung, Carl G. *Symbols of Transformation*. Translated by R. F. C. Hull. New York: Pantheon Books Inc., 1956. (Copyright 1956 by Bollingen Foundation, Inc., New York, and published for the Bollingen Foundation by Pantheon Books).

45. Kardiner, Abraham. *The Individual and his Society. The Psychodynamics of Primitive Social Organization*. New York: Columbia University Press, 1939.

46. Langer, Marie. *Maternidad y sexo. Estudio psicoanalítico y psicosomático*. Buenos Aires: Editorial Nova, 1951.
47. Lebon, Gustave. *L'homme et les sociétés*. 2 vols. Paris: J. Roschild, Editeur, 1881.
48. Magalhães, Basílio de. *O folclore do Brasil*. 1928; rpt. with a collection of 81 popular tales organized by Dr. João da Silva Campos. Rio de Janeiro: Imprensa Nacional, 1939.
49. Malinowski, Bronislaw. *The Sexual Life of Savages In North Western Melanesia*. Preface by Havelock Ellis. New York: Halcyon House, 1929.
50. Mello Morales Filho. *Festas e tradições populares do Brasil*. 3rd revised edition by Luis da Câmara Cascudo. Rio de Janeiro: F. Briguiet and Cia, Editôres, 1946.
51. Monteiro Lobato. "Fabulas." Vol. XIV, *Obras Completas*. São Paulo: Editôra Brasiliense Limitada, 1946.
52. Mullahy, Patrick. *Oedipus, Myth and Complex*. New York: Grove Press, Inc., 1948.
53. Nina-Rodrigues, Raymundo. *Os Africanos no Brasil*. 3rd edition, revised and with a preface by Homero Pires. São Paulo: Companhia Editôra Nacional, 1945.
54. Ortiz, Fernando. "La tragedia de los ñáñigos." *Cuadernos Americanos*, 9, No. 4 (1950), 79–101.
55. Pôrto-Carrero, J. P. *A psicologia profunda ou psicanálise*, 3rd revised edition. Rio de Janeiro: Ed. Guanabara, 1934.
56. Ramos, Arthur. *O folklore negro do Brasil. Demopsicologia e psicanálise*. Rio de Janeiro: Civilização Brasileira, S. A., 1935.
57. Ramos, Arthur. *Estudos de Folk-lore*. Preface by Roger Bastide. Rio de Janeiro: Livraria da Casa do Estudante do Brasil, 1952.
58. Ramos, Arthur. *Freud, Adler, Jung. Ensaios de Psicanálise orthodoxa e herética*. Preface by Afrânio Peixoto. Rio de Janeiro: Ed. Guanabara, 1933.
59. Ramos, Arthur. *Introdução à Psicologia Social*. Rio de Janeiro: Livraria José Olympio, 1936.
60. Ramos, Arthur. *The Negro in Brazil*. Translated by Richard Pattee. Washington D. C.: The Associated Publishers, Inc., 1951.
61. Ramos, Arthur. "A organização dual entre os indios brasileiros." Thesis presented during the competition for the Chair of Anthropology and Ethnography of the National Faculty of Philosophy, Rio de Janeiro, 1945.
62. Ramos, Arthur. *Primitivo e loucura*. Dissertation for the Degree of Doctor of Medicine, Bahia, 1926.
63. Ramos, Arthur. *Psiquiatria e psicanálise*. Rio de Janeiro: Civilização Brasileira. 1933.
64. Rojas, Nerio. *El diablo y la loucura y otros ensayos*. Buenos Aires: Libreria El Ateneo Editorial, 1951.
65. Senet, Rodolfo. *Las Estoglosias. Contribución al estudio del lenguaje*. Madrid: Daniel Jorro, Editor, 1911.

66. Uchôa, Severino. "O jôgo do bicho. Folklore." *Revista Época.* Aracaju: Mensagem dos Novos de Sergipe, 1949.
67. Van Gennep, Arnold. *Manuel de folklore français contemporaine.* Vol. I. Paris: Editions Auguste Picard, 1943.
68. Viqueira, Carmen and Palerm, Angel. "Alcoholismo, brujería y homicidio en dos comunidades rurales de México." *America Indigena,* 14 (Jan. 1954), 7–36.
69. Wortis, Joseph. *Soviet Psychiatry.* Baltimore: The Williams and Wilkins Co., 1950.

Index

Abraham, Karl, on dreams and myths, 25

anal libido. *See* libido

animism. *See* religion

anxiety, 61–62, 75, 176–179

Bastide, Roger, on capitalism and anal eroticism, 102; on psychoanalytical sociology, 40–41

birth, fantasies, 180–185; meaning of water, 161

Canal-Feijoo, Bernardo, folklore in Argentina, 41–42

Carneiro, Édison, on dialectical materialism, 40

castration complex, 60, 61; and anxiety, 62, 176–179; symbol, 173

censorship, of the unconscious, 70

children, erotic wishes, 56; excrement, 52; sexual curiosity, 59–61; sexual pleasure, 50; sucking, 51, 57

coitus, 128, 191

collective unconscious, 27, 76–84

compensation, principle of, 71

conscious, meaning of, 71, 72, 73, 74, 75

cross, feast of the, 191–195

death, 151

dreams, and myths, 25; Nietzsche's ideas of, 79–80; prediction of, 67; symbolism, 23–24, 43, 64–68

Ellis, Havelock, and anal libido, 98–100

embolalia, 88–92

erotogenic zones, 50, 51; genitals, 55

Evil Father. *See* father

Evil Mother. *See* mother

excrements, children play with, 101; sacred, 100

fairy tales, 24; anal libido, 103, 104–107, 107–108; about birth, 181–185; Evil Father, 157–158; 159; Evil Mother, 162–163, 167; about the tortoise, 196

faith, 115

family, Malinowski's theory of, 28–31

father, child's sexual object, 56; Evil, 156–161, 177, 179; symbolism, 55, 146, 155

fetishism, 124–129, 192

fire, symbolizes libido, 155

food, symbolic, 192; totemic, 132–133

Freud, Sigmund, on animism, 191; and anxiety, 61–62; the conscious and the unconscious, 68–75; criticized by Wortis, 34–35; his errors, 32–33; infantile sexuality, 59–61; and libido, 48–53; on magic, 113–115; on narcissism, 53; Oedipus complex, 53–59; phylogenetic symbolism, 23–24; seen